Corpus Christi Writers 2022

Expanded Edition

Edited by

William Mays

For more information contact
William Mays
Mays Publishing.
Books@mayspublishing.com

Cover Design by Alexis Mays Harborth

Copy Editor Tom Murphy

Special Thanks to Joseph Wilson

Printed in the United States of America

ISBN
978-1-7334696-4-7

Introduction

The *Corpus Christi Writers* series strives to present diverse views and perspectives that, taken as a whole, reflect what people in this community are thinking. Many writers from previous anthologies return to this fifth book in the series, and many new writers join them. Youthful exuberance coexists with polished style. The themes vary and express the unique viewpoints of the writers. Chupacabras and talking animals take a hiatus this year, while Port Aransas figures prominently. Teeth make a strong appearance, and one story is told from the perspective of a can of paint.

In previous anthologies, we included photos and art that illustrated or amplified the selections or the writing process. Here, we are showcasing the rich and diverse work of visual artists from South Texas because they are a vital part of the creative environment. The images range from traditional to abstract. The Kindle version contains color images. This Expanded Edition includes additional writing included in the Kindle version, but not in the earlier print versions.

Much of the content from each of the anthologies migrates to MaysPublishing.com. This website now has rich content that rotates daily and draws an average of a thousand visitors a month. It links directly to the websites of the authors and artists. We invite anyone anywhere in the world to join the community. In addition to showcasing outstanding work, we strive to become a trusted source for people looking for quality writing, particularly flash fiction, poetry, and works that combine words and images.

For full bios and more information on the writers in CCW2022, please go to MaysPublishing.com

First lines by William Mays

Table of Contents

Alan Berecka

Alan Berecka was the Poet Laureate of Corpus Christi from February 2017 - February 2019. His work has appeared in such publications as *Red River Review*, *Texas Review*, *The Christian Century*, *Windhover*, *Ruminate*, *St. Peter's B-List* and *Oklahoma Poems...And Their Poets*.

Blue-Collar Heaven

My father never got a paid day off—
no sick days, no holidays, not even
Christmas, so he worked on every Eve,
and birthday, dragged himself to work
with fevers, and stitches, often over
my mother's protests because, "The God-
damned bills won't pay themselves."

His tin knocker's union had a healthy
strike fund, so he never voted to ratify
a single contract, no matter how
reasonable the terms, no matter
if Jesus Christ himself returned to Utica
as a union boss and preached on the value
of ratification, my old man's mind
would have remain unchanged,
even if he knew his thumbs down
would place his back-pew Catholic soul
in peril because nothing he could imagine
came closer to paradise than sitting
on a cheap lawn chair in his backyard
on a weekday afternoon while nursing
a cold brew and watching his grass grow
all the while knowing that a fat check
from the union sat in his bank account
answering his most basic of prayers.

Mrs. Robinson Forgets Joe DiMaggio

Where have you gone
Walter Cronkite?

Our nation turns its
bleary eyes to you.

Wishes you'd show us "The way
it is" signing off just once more,

show us the way to see a united
truth based on facts that count

help us relearn, that these facts
differ from my opinion and yours

remind us again that Jesus loves
us all more than we can know.

We look to you Uncle Walter
to revive our gasping body politic

unresponsive turning blue on the floor,
breathe life into the common good

our one nation once united
by more than the vainest

of notions, our newest creed—
"Yeah, but, what's in it for me?"

What's that you say Mrs. Robinson?
Uncle Walter's left and gone away.

Hey, hey, hey.
Woe, woe, woe.

Seashore by John Morris

Alisa Hope Wagner

Alisa Hope Wagner is an award-winning author, editor and publisher of over 30 books. She married her high school sweetheart, and together they raise their three children in a Christ-centered home.

The Hat Shoppe

Illustration Albert Morales

Devon jumped from the final step of the city bus. He didn't care what the other passengers thought about his childish gesture. He had waited for this day most of his life. He had achieved something his family had never accomplished. He had graduated from college. In a few days, he would walk the stage and take hold of his best life, but first he had a promise to keep.

He looked around at the tall buildings of the city. When he was a boy, the important sidewalks and bustling buildings jeered at him. Now, the sidewalks would bow, and buildings would stand at attention. His mother had worked in the city all his life, cleaning rooms of elegant hotels with their ballrooms and swimming pools. Hotels never closed. Suits still worked and vacationers still played.

And his mother had cleaned until she became worn and sick.

Once, when he was eight years old, he came to the city with her on a school holiday. She pointed out a man who wore a sleek grey suit with leather shoes and a felt hat. He looked like he belonged in the city, and Devon felt out of place in his jeans, t-shirt and tennis shoes.

"You see that man?" his mom asked.

"Yes, Mamma," he answered, noticing that the hotel seemed to lean away from the man in awe.

"He's a businessman. You can be like him someday, but you have to get your college degree. Do you understand?"

The boy quickly moved his gaze from the businessman to his mother's serious stare. He felt the weight of her words, and they dropped into his soul like handfuls of acorn seeds that scattered the dusty ground of his school's playground. He nodded solemnly and stared back at the man in the suit. He was stepping into a shiny SUV. "I like his hat, Mama. When I become a businessman, can I get a hat like his?"

His mother gently nudged her calloused finger into the backpack he held. "You can get any hat you want. I overheard him asking the concierge where he could purchase a nice felt hat. They sent him to the hat shop only a few blocks from the hotel. It has been there for almost a hundred years, and it has many hats to choose from. The hats from that shop are very well made, yet very expensive. I'll take you there after work, and you can look through the windows. Would you like that?"

The boy nodded his head fervently.

"Okay," his mom said, standing. "Now we must go. I can't punch in late."

Tension stole Devon's childhood memory, as the shadow of the hotel fell across the section of city where the bus let him out. He could have gotten off at the next stop and been closer to the hat shop, but he needed the hotel to take note. Devon levelled his chin and puffed out his chest while swinging his arms and legs in long, purposeful strides. The next time that hotel saw him, he would have a college degree in his hands, not a ratty, old backpack.

As Devon reached the windows of the hat shop, he hesitated. He had never walked into the window-framed image of fashionably flaunted hats before. The scene seemed to him more of a painted illusion, but it would momentarily become a firsthand reality. A sun-faded sign that read, "Selling Hats for 100 Years," winked at him from one of the glass-pained sections of the door. He promptly groped for the bills in the right pocket of his slacks. He worked on campus to supplement the scholarships and grants he had received. Each month, he'd save every crumb of coinage that fell at his table. Finally, he exchanged the scraps of cash for five fresh Benjamins rolled up like brass knuckles in his pocket ready to break the ceiling of lack over his life.

He could have waited until his first paycheck to secure his hat. The college career services helped him receive a paid internship with a bank thanks to his minor in finance, but paychecks were for practical things, like rent and food. This purchase, however, was a declaration to the universe that his will would rewrite the unfolding scroll of time. He would buy the businessman's felt hat and walk the sidewalks that once shooed him away. Then busy buildings would open their arms to him, but only a hat from this shop would do. His mom had said so, and she stressed that they were expensive. Determinedly, Devon grabbed the curved brass door handle of the shop and stepped inside.

Devon's skin soaked up the smells of the hat shop, absorbing the aromas of wealth and affluence. If ever he designed his own cologne, it would smell like this moment, and he would douse his suit daily in its self-assured essence. An elderly man appeared next to him, and his smile stretched across his aged cheeks into his wrinkled eyes. "My name is Eleazar, but my customers and friends call me Ellie. I am the owner of this hat shop. It has been in my family for over a century. I can see that you are a young man in need of a good hat, and I am ready to assist you in that endeavor. Our hats are each hand-made with the finest natural materials. You will not find better workmanship with more integrity on this side of the continent."

The intimidation Devon had unknowingly carried into the hat shop dissolved, and he withdrew his right hand from his pocket of money and offered it to Mr. Ellie, the hat shop owner. He had never questioned the cost of the hats. His mom had said that they were the best, and he took her convictions by faith. However, the shop owner's statement of quality added a measure of assurance to his acquisition. "Good afternoon, Mr. Ellie. My name is Devon DeWitt, and I just earned my college degree. I'm here to purchase a felt hat, so I can begin my career in the city."

The old shop owner took Devon's hand into his calloused palm and gave it a few good shakes. Something about his fingers reminded Devon of his mother, and he knew more than ever that he was meant to be there. The rest of his life began here, and suddenly, the weight of his momentary choice fell on him like four years of learning squeezed into a single, dense second. The rows of arranged hats called out to him, and the five-hundred-dollar bills in his pocket burned. Perspiration gathered on his forehead, and an image of staining his new felt hat with sweat stabbed his chest with fear.

The old shop owner seemed to notice the change in Devon's countenance, and he nodded with understanding. Then he placed his calloused hand on Devon's shoulder and peered into his anxious expression. "Don't you worry one bit," the old owner affirmed. "I'll help you find the right fit and hat. I've been helping my customers for a very long time. There are indeed many hats to choose from and lots of styles and colors to consider, but we can whittle down the choices a great deal once I get your size and you tell me what you are looking for."

An air of relief filled Devon's lungs and his heavy chest lifted lightly. "Mr. Ellie, I'm looking for a felt hat, and when I see it, I will know."

The old shop owner gave a meaningful nod. "I believe you will. Here," he said, as a measuring tape unfurled from his fingers. "Let me measure you for the perfect fit."

Devon leaned his head forward. He hadn't noticed the measuring tape in the shop owner's hand, but he was an expert hat maker and knew what he was doing. Devon felt Mr. Ellie place the tape's end above his left ear and wrap the length of it around the circumference of his head just across his eyebrows. Then he released the loose end and pinched the tape at the right measurement.

"Yep, just what I thought, but I wanted to be sure. Now follow me," Mr. Ellie said. The shop owner made his way into the middle of the showroom and waited for Devon to join him. Then he pointed to the far left. "Those are flat caps," he said. Then his pointed hand veered to the right, inch by inch, as he listed the rest of the hats. "Those are buckets hats. And those are bakerboy caps. Next are trilby hats and then Panama hats. And finally," he said, motioning to the far right. "Those are fedoras. There are different designs within each collection, but you can at least make your way to the section of the store you favor most. Within each collection, we have different materials—felt, leather, tweed, linen, straw, silk, and more—but since you want felt, your choice will be even easier to make."

Devon realized there was more to the word *hat* than he had considered, but once he saw the shelves of fedoras, he knew where he needed to look. "Definitely the fedoras," Devon said confidently.

"I thought just as much. Fedoras have a feel for the city. Why don't you make your way over there and examine each felt fedora closely? They may look similar from a distance, but I assure you they each have a distinctive design and hue. There are no wrong choices. Now that we know your size and desired collection, the rest is a matter of opinion and taste."

Devon waivered. He had all but forgotten about price. "I must also mention, although I have saved for many years, I do have a budget of no more than five hundred dollars."

"I respect your budget," Mr. Ellie assured. "Some folks come in here ill-prepared to hear the price. They either get angry and storm out of my shop or they become embarrassed and apologize. However, your budget should cover almost any felt hat in the store, save the top hats on the racks behind the register. I didn't mention those because they didn't fit your need."

Devon gave a low laugh with relief. "No, I will not be looking at top hats for a while. If you don't mind, I will look at your selection."

"Take your time," Mr. Ellie said. "I'll be checking my inventory-list behind the register. Let me know if you need anything."

Devon watched the old hat shop owner step behind the counter of his register. He eyed the top hats lining the wall behind him. No, he didn't need one of those. He turned his gaze to the rows of elegant fedoras and made his way to their location. Mr. Ellie was correct. There were many felt fedoras to choose from, and he could envision the businessman wearing each one. He reached his hand toward the taupe-colored fedora with a pinched shaped crown and narrow brim, but he stopped abruptly when a hissing voice came from behind.

"Are you sure that is the perfect one?" the tall man sneered. He wore a dark-colored fedora that reflected the celling lights of the showroom. It had an exaggerated pinched crown, forming the two points of the letter "M" and an extra wide brim that shaded the man's face entirely.

"Mr. Ellie and I decided that I should choose my hat from here. I want a felt fedora, and this is my selection."

The man scoffed. "Why felt? What a boring material. My silk fedora glows."

"I am a young man. I want a hat that will last me," Devon said, trying to dismiss the man.

"Why would the owner even limit you here when there are hundreds of choices," the tall man pressed, spreading his arms like he owned the shop. "You cannot make this decision lightly. The price is too hefty for just any old hat."

Devon stepped back. He had been working toward this decision for years, and he didn't want to choose incorrectly. He did find the man's hat attractive. He looked to his left, and the other appealing collection of hats beckoned him—every color, every size, every design and every function bombarded his thoughts with what-ifs. He turned back to the man to seek further advice, but he was stunned to see that the man's silk, cream fedora was now replaced with a checkered, tweed flat cap that flopped across his face like a mourning veil.

"Did you change hats?" Devon asked in disbelief.

"Well, of course I did!" the man hissed. "Why would I want to be stuck with the same hat day after day, week after week and year after year when there are so many hats to choose from?"

Devon did find the man's hat intriguing. Then another hat captured Devon's side-gaze. It was one of the trilby hats. It was the same taupe color as the fedora he had picked out, but this one had a leather band around the bottom of the crown. "I do like that one also," he said, pointing. "It looks a lot like the fedora except the crown is not so pinched." He closed his eyes, remembering the businessman from when he was young. His hat had been a fedora, but he didn't have to match it exactly.

The trilby would be nice.

Devon turned back to the tall man to get his opinion, but now he wore an oversized, linen bucket hat that hung over his ears and eyes like a stemless, grey mushroom. That hat truly excited him. "You changed your hat again!"

A sly smile curled along the man's lips like a greasy mustache. "I don't keep the same hat for long. It bores me, so I must have something new."

Devon glanced back at the fedoras in front of him. The leather ones looked nice; although, they probably cost a lot more that the felt fedoras. He could see if Mr. Ellie would allow him time to pay the rest with his first paycheck. "What about leather?" Devon asked the tall man.

When he turned back, he was unable to suppress his shock as the man now wore a towering crimson top hat. Devon had to suppress the urge to take the red hat for himself. "You changed it again!"

"Yes, and you can too. You shouldn't have to stick with just one hat. You can have any hat you choose. I have loads of credit as this store. Just put them in my name, and you can pay me back over time."

Devon's chest clinched as images of hats scattered his mind like cards flying out of a bad shuffle. He looked toward the cash register to find Mr. Ellie, but the shop owner was nowhere in sight. Suddenly, he no longer trusted the tall man's advice. He felt anxious and confused, like he was drowning under an endless pile of would-be hats. "No," Devon declared, directing his thoughts. "I will pick from the selection that Mr. Ellie and I already agreed upon." He looked back at the taupe felt fedora he had examined first. He did like it, but it was a little bland.

"Would you like me to put a band around it?" the old shop keeper asked.

Devon looked around. The tall man was gone, and Mr. Ellie stood at his side.

"Yes, I would like that. Will it be leather?" Devon asked.

"The leather band would go over your budget, but I have a fabric band that would look just as nice," Mr. Ellie said.

Devon took hold of his new hat. "Yes, that will be perfect."

"I'll box it up for you," the old owner said, taking the hat from Devon's hands.

"I'll take the box but don't pack up the hat. I want to wear it out," Devon said.

"I think that is a fine idea," the shop owner agreed. "You have chosen well."

When Devon exited the shop, a sunray reflecting off a city window shined on him like a spotlight. The sidewalk became his stage and the buildings his audience. He tilted the fedora with a gesture of greeting.

"Welcome to the city, Devon DeWitt!" the traffic roared.

Alyanna Mena

Many live to work; Alyanna works to live. She loves reading, painting, drawing, and singing. She thanks her friends and family for always being there to support her and thanks those who have recently departed while keeping them close in her heart.

I Am But a Formulation

Do you know what it's like to feel used? I am used every day in different ways. I'll explain later.

While most people wake, drink their morning caffeinated beverage, and go to their 9-5, I stay encapsulated in a decorated can. Humans have free range to roam, but that is not the case. I'm encased! Depending on the living you humans make, I can be quite expensive (or cheap). People come from different backgrounds, and I'm used by all of them. I live in and through everything. I stain. However, I don't make an appearance unless I have to. Honey, I'm actually quite shy. I can't control it either, so please forgive me. There's a puppeteer at play, and I am their doll.

Remember I told you I would explain? Riddle you not.

I'm paint. That stuff your kid would smear the wall with, what Picasso used to create masterpieces, licked on clay, and what is forgotten and left under your bed for years. I've probably been on your fridge at one point but like I said, I'm diverse. Everyone knows what it is and where they can purchase me. I'm not just any paint; I'm black paint. In theory there is nothing darker than me, but there is. It's how being a color makes me feel. I'm an inanimate object but part of a collective consciousness. To others, I am nothing yet everything at the same time. Not every color is as humble. But I am the color that darkens other colors. Do you know how that feels? Mix myself with anything, and I will run my dark veins into their being and attach myself like a parasite. I suppose I could be the absence of color yet still one, white. Mix me up with him, and I turn grey. But that's their story to tell. Here's mine.

You humans are like colors too. Everyone I've been with has been different. Sure, age plays a factor as to where you are in the world, but all of you want the same thing. That meaning you yearn for to make it day by day fascinates me. I am a color, and that is my purpose. The only time I'm needed is to mend or create. I've come to accept that is what I will do for the rest of my existence. Humans are ravenous creatures that can't sit still. Nothing is ever good enough. My good friend, Time, has a good story about that, but it isn't about them right now.

I understand wanting to be more. I never chose to become a color. Physically, there isn't a way to make me more interesting. You get what you get, and that's that. It's all about how I'm used. That is my point from earlier. Honestly, there's a certain rush to being used spontaneously. I've been at football stadiums, museums, soccer fields, schools, homes, cathedrals, aquariums, and much more. I've seen so much so from an outsider's perspective; let me enlighten you.

There are milestones to being a color. First container, first user, first conversion, first mixture, first creation, and first to be used up. There is a bittersweet feeling once you get tossed into the trash. I thank humans for their time and energy. Not everyone is artistic, but it's the thought that counts. I get to be a part of their creative process, and that's how legacies are made in the color world. Similarly, human legacies are also creations, but at least you can reproduce.

Even paint has a tendency to taint my dear. We all do.

Alyssa Outhwaite

Alyssa Outhwaite is a graduate student at Texas A&M University-Corpus Christi. Her love of writing began in middle school where she often spent her days creating short stories with her sisters and friends. She was inspired to write "Only if" while struggling with the demands of getting a Ph.D. and believed her feelings would resonate with others juggling happiness and "success."

Only if

Sneezing, wheezing, coughing, hacking
Still I lay there typing tapping
Keyboard strokes, no time for napping
Pushing through pain, my strength sapping.

Eyes watering, breathing ragged
Forcing forward feeling haggard
Pages frayed my corners jagged
To stop is lazy? I'm staggered.

To rest, to sleep, to breathe's a crime
Too many things, not enough time
Repeats all day, my mantra chime,
"If I had more hours, I'd be fine."

It's a lie, I'd fill each with more
And endless time? I'd be a whore
Selling my soul for open doors
How else do I move forward?

Enough, *enough*! I want to rant
Where is the time for me? I pant
The rest, they sleep, and breathe! I can't?
Is this the prize ambition grants?

Pressing on to be efficient,
Perfect model of persistence,
But will alone is not sufficient
Blunted axes are deficient.

I should stop to sharpen my tool

To restore the mind, rest is fuel
These seem like lies, and I a fool
For wanting breaks to be a rule.

You'd think stopping would be easy
To care less, be light and breezy,
But it's so hard I feel queasy.
Surrender makes me uneasy.

Fear of failure keeps me going
Climbing high no weakness showing
With each new height my dread growing.
Sure to fall but there's no slowing.

At the top I toss a token
Wishing, praying words unspoken
From this nightmare to be woken
Yet terror remains unbroken.

At the end, when my time has come
I hope, of all the things I've done,
That regret not have the largest sum.
Maybe. Only if change has won.

Azrael Montoya

Azrael Montoya has lived in Corpus Christi his whole life. He believes that life is about making a series of choices and hoping for some luck sometimes.

Here I Am

Here I am in the city
drinking so I can fall in the street.
I'm shooting drugs so I can live forever.

Here is her chart that lists everything but not the past reality of her vibrance and flesh.
Here I am wondering.
I'm not going anywhere.
Everybody lives and everybody dies.

Her coma froze me in place.
I'm in trouble.
I need to drink some more and more.
While the coma and machine turned her from real to dripping water and sand on the hill.

Here I am still the same. Love for the woman and man won't stop the coma and the machine from helping end the race

Love You

It was hard to find you.
I really had to try.
You drove me to work and I was
thankful. Your smile was beautiful and
luminous like daisies in the field.
Your laugh was like a beautiful wet shark.

I said all
the time, I
love you.
I love you.
I really did.

Touching your body all time was smooth as a record. We kissed for long periods of time and it was greatly appreciated. It will go down in history.

I love you.
I love you.
I needed you.

You put on your blue uniform to go fight in the war for the spiritual world.
You always followed the prescriptions in your zenned up journal.
Our focus on love was like an Act of Congress.
It was powerful and atomic.
Its very essence sure of itself.

Then the other better man came with his gun in the air to get your
attention.
And finally you left me in my house with clutter to be back no more.

Blu Chapa

I am a young poet who informs students at my school that they aren't alone. It's going to be okay no matter what.

Brain

My brain…
Shut the fuck up please!
The constant thought of
They're mad at me.
I did something wrong.
Help them; they helped you.
Save them; they need you.
You have to prove your worth, so they'll stay.
Please stay!
Don't leave!
Please don't!
I've been alone and in the dark before.
It's sad… scary,
so don't leave me alone.
Please.

In My Thoughts

As I sit in my thoughts thinking.
My eyes start to fill with a water.
As I think about what happened.
What happened long ago.
But it still hurts.
I thought I've healed from my pain.
I thought I was okay.
But I'm so broken.
The smallest problem
Shatters me more,
I wonder how many pieces I'm in now.

Carol Mays

Carol Mays wrote *Nevins*, the story of a talking cat, and the sequel, *Nevins 2: Saving the Junkyard.* She also wrote *103 Crazy Ideas for Surviving Suburbia* and co-wrote *Escape from Sunny Shores* with her husband.

Trailer Life

Call me *"trailer trash." I don't care!*

Let me pour you another cup of coffee. Drag your chair closer and listen with an open mind. I am going to tell you how wonderful a trailer is compared to traditional homes. If you find that your bills are piling up, and that your home is sucking you dry,then maybe this is something you need to consider.

I firmly believe that the best life is a house on wheels! I could list more than a hundred reasons why a trailer is better than a house of any kind. Here's a brief history. Trailers, in America, are a modern version of the pioneer days when settlers crossed the west with their possessions. They symbolize freedom, hope, and independence. While Americans are not the first to invent the house on wheels, we will not stop re-inventing trailers to suit our modern needs. Now, let me say here, I'm not trying to convince you to quit your job, sell everything you have, and buy a trailer. What I want to achieve is an awareness that trailers have as much or more value than a stationary home and are deserving of the same respect you give the country clubs across America. I know what you're going to say. The pioneers crossed the west to build cabins and *settle*. But, I think if they could see what we're going through in our houses, they would stay in their wagons. In fact, they would circle the wagons permanently, creating the first RV park!

I love my teardrop twelve- foot trailer more than my three-thousand-square-foot brick home. In fact, if my husband and I ever divorced—God forbid—I would *fight him* for the trailer. He can have the house and everything in it. Except the cat. But, that's another story. The cat doesn't like the trailer. He's a terrible snob. I know I sound ungrateful about the house, but I'm really not. You see, the house sucks *in a lot of different ways*—and most of all it sucks the life out of me. For example, I could spend anywhere from four to twelve hours cleaning. It depends on who has visited us and how long I let things go—which I never do because I'm a total clean freak. I purchase all kinds of mops, vacuum cleaners, cleansers etc. to complete this annoying task. The trailer on the other hand?

No problem! I can drive it to the nearest car wash and wait behind the guy cleaning his boat. I can use all the equipment there and then, treat myself to a burger—which is generally right next door to the car wash or across the street. And, no, I can't go out after cleaning the house. Burger places are far away from the suburbs and besides, I'm passed out after all that hard work.

Oh, and best of all, I bet your house doesn't' smell like a new car every time you walk in it. My trailer? It has that *new car* smell all the time. I invited my snobby friend over to my trailer for a visit and that was her first response. It was truly nice of her. She's right. It always has that new car smell.

Here's some more cool things about trailers. You know how people spend a fortune on surround sound stereos? Well, in a metal trailer all you need is a regular radio, because the sound just bounces around. Oh, and cooking is with propane. Talk about fast! Somehow, everything you make tastes better. Eggs are farm fresh and fluffier, and coffee is bold and real—like cowboy/pioneer real, and cheap, not overpriced Starbucks stuffy flavor. You do have to open all the windows and the door when you cook in a trailer or the smoke alarm will go off for no reason, but that's a small thing compared to the great meal you get. Someone once asked me if the trailer was comfortable to sleep in. What an odd question. It's the best rest ever! There's nothing like the comfort of those vinyl foam seats and fresh cotton sheets covered with a scrap quilt. Just think about this: the dinette transforms into a queen size bed, so it's like breakfast in bed, everyday! If that's not country-club life then, I don't know what is.

You look like you're running out of coffee. Wine? Sure, I've got some wine. I'll get it.

Now, where was I? Oh, yeah. Trailers offer freedom. You see, with a trailer, I can live wherever I want. And, when I can't stand my neighbor, or the area is having bad weather,-I can move. Try doing that with a house! You might ask where can you go. After all, a lot of trailer parks have gotten a bad reputation over the years. And, yes, I am sure there are those that need improvement. But, there are plenty of neighborhoods across America that are just as bad if not worse. There are all kinds of trailer parks and just like neighborhoods, houses, apartments, condos, and townhouses each one caters to the needs of the residents. If you are over the age of fifty-five for example, you might want a seniors-only park. They have fun bingo and card games, potluck dinners and other social stuff. They offer lower prices for fixed income. And, like anything else, if you are not happy, you can just drive your house down the road. You don't even need to pack up.

Here's another thing to consider. Got rats in your attic? In a house, you need an exterminator, a roofer, and a carpenter just for starters in a home. In a trailer? Trap the rat, spray foam the hole, and drive away from the area. *Problem solved!*

I guess I should address what many people find most concerning about a trailer: the sewer system—if you can call it that. It's really just some hoses. My advice: buy gloves to deal with the "*black water.*" All trailer parks have a place to connect your sewer hose. If you are off-roading- meaning you are in the middle of nowhere- then, you can't do that. You would have to go to a dump station. Get the gloves.

Oh! And, here's another thought! Many homeowners suffer with foundation issues. It costs a fortune to fix, but *not in a trailer.* Simply, air the tires and crank the stabilizers on the front and sides of the trailer or drive away to more stable land. It's like that Dr. Seuss book, *Oh, The Places You Will Go.* I'd like to add you will park and park and park. You will even park in a park!

So, to answer your question: where is my trailer parked now? In our driveway. Yes, in the suburbs. I don't care what the neighbors or the HOA think about it. The HOA can take me to court for all I care. I pay the taxes on my house, so I can park my truck and trailer in the driveway if I want. Besides, my trailer is so small you can't even see it in the private alley. I think HOA's are un-American! Don't you?!

So, this brings me to my big plan. Want to know it?

You really like that wine, don't you? I know I'm intense, but bear with me. Oh, you want to just drink it straight from the bottle. Good thing I didn't buy the box kind.

Anyway, I want to generate a petition to dismantle all HOAs. Then, get the city to rezone all neighborhoods so that homeowners can choose to demolish their homes—you know when they have rats, foundation, and/or renovation problems or they just hate them—and replace them with a shiny new trailer!

Oh, wait. You shouldn't drink wine that fast. You finished the whole bottle! Wait! Where are you going? Hey, I'm not done telling you all my ideas! I'm just getting started. Oh, and one more thing, when you see someone on the road driving a trailer—*slow down!* It's annoying to be tailgated when you are towing your home.

Remember this: *it's the trailer life for me!*

Chuck Etheridge

A self-proclaimed desert from El Paso, Chuck Etheridge teaches English at Texas A&M University-Corpus Christi. His poetry, fiction, and creative non-fiction have been published in a variety of reviews and books, and he has written two plays that have been produced.

Corona of Thorns

No palm leaves
On Palm Sunday
No crosses folded
Out of palm leaves

Missing the
Annual chance
To practice that skill
Learned in childhood

No Maundy Thursday
Washing of the feet
That intimate ritual
Reminding us to serve others

No Good Friday vigil,
Bleary eyed
In the wee hours
Awaiting the resurrection

No sunrise service
Sleepy eyed but joyful
No breaking of the Easter fast
At the local diner

No Easter egg hunt
No kids
Dressed in their finest
Trolling for loot

No visit
From my son
Who lives
In another city

This last, a bitter pill
No matter where the family has gone
We've always managed
To gather at Easter

Corona means "crown"
A very different
Crown of thorns
Than the one Easter celebrates

I know that much remains
The season is real
The promise of hope
Needed now more than ever

New rituals
Church live streamed over Facebook
Book of Common Prayer on the cell phone
Trying to kneel on the living room floor

We will still have
Our barbecue,
Will video chat
Easter dinner

With our distant son,
Will have chocolate eggs
A social distance
Easter egg hunt

Made perhaps more special
More urgent
By the bad news
Around us

No Church in Chones

Before Covid-19
Getting myself and the child
To church dressed
In slacks and dress shirt
Was doable

Routine
Effortless
Now, in the Time of Social Distance
We struggle
To get everyone up

And to the living room
By 10:30
We "attend" church
On Facebook Live
Book of Common prayer

On cell phones
No slacks or shirt collars in sight
Splayed across the couch
Slumped in recliners
Tee shirts and shorts

Communion is crackers
And blackberry soda
Hymns are off key
Prayers are mumbled
An occasional sermon-time nap

But we still have standards,
One commandment, inviolable
You can't appear in just your underwear
No church in chones
You have to wear pants

Dog on the Seashore by Cynthia Giery

Christian Garduno

Christian Garduno's work can be read in over 100 literary magazines. He is the recipient of the 2019 national Willie Morris Award for Southern Poetry, a Finalist in the 2020-2021 Tennessee Williams & New Orleans Writing Contest, and a Finalist in the 2021 Julia Darling Memorial Poetry Prize. He lives and writes along the South Texas coast with his wonderful wife Nahemie and young son Dylan.

General Delivery

I was on the house-phone in the kitchen
you were looking out over the Mendenhall Glacier
watching three bear-cubs romping below
seems like you said that for an hour

It'd be a good time for you to swim back to shore for sure
I got your telegram last week, I keep it hidden away in my composition book

Giovanni's back along the coast
I tried sending him something general delivery
Lord knows if he ever got it
he never writes back anymore

Me & Geems went to see The Virginian earlier this summer
he's living as high on the hog as he ever has
even got his own little railway station
doing mighty fine indeed

It'd be a good time for you to swim back to shore for sure
I got your telegram last week, I keep it hidden away in my composition book

Thanks for the $100 you sent last month
your timing was impeccable
I took young Dylan for a cheeseburger and strawberry shakes
I'll wire you back when I'm flush

Vanity Press

We drank the moonshine down
as the moon shined down
and saw no irony in it whatsoever
that's how it was forever
it's only now I see
how it was pressing in on my vanity
but it was another time
back then, I didn't mind

you got me in italics
& it feels alright
it feels right

If I could copy and paste those nights
I'd have them right back here again
life doesn't wait for if's
that's one thing you learn
as your youth burns
and leaves you with salt and pepper in your hair
I close my eyes so tight that everything turns white
so I toss back my head and drink to you tonight

you got me in italics
& it feels alright
it feels right

You stay the same, it's only your state of mind that changes
you bring me your old chords, now I'm singing a new song
the world isn't much when you live and love in a small town
when your lover cries, it's easy to drown
it used to press in on my vanity, but now I see
it's just the way I used to be, I make better mistakes now
I didn't like getting over you
I would have liked the older you

Clara Isabel Tamez

Clara Tamez was born in Corpus Christi, Texas in 1994. Her love of literature began as a child reading Emily Dickinson's *Poetry for Young People*. She has traveled through Greece, Italy, France, Malta, Iceland, Scotland, and England and spent most of her childhood writing songs and filling up sketchbooks. She holds a Bachelor of Arts degree from the University of the Incarnate Word in English and a Master of Fine Arts degree in Creative Writing from Kingston University London. She currently resides in San Antonio, Texas

The Just Before

"Would you still love me if I didn't have teeth?"

"Did you wake up with them gone or did you get into an accident?" Jaydon's voice sounds a little hollow as it always does over the prison phone line. "Or were you born without them somehow?" He laughs and I imagine the curl of his lips as he pictures a me with no teeth or the laugh I would have gotten if I told him I had no hair, or had been magically transformed into a chicken. I loved the laugh I would have gotten with that one.

"All of the above. Start with me waking up without them."

"It would be freaky. I'd be more worried about the trauma inflicted on you, waking up with puddles of teeth in your lap."

"Hah! I imagined they just disappeared. Now what if I got into an accident and they all fell out?"

"That'd be some accident."

Questions that used to be for fun are now a welcome, necessary distraction for both of us. I give him scenarios and he goes through as many as he can in fifteen minutes. Sometimes, we get thirty, if no other inmates are waiting.

These calls are a lot better than they used to be. The first one was: "Luna, you need to help my mom with Ada."

I didn't want to at first. That was what he did, and he would continue doing it. Until I heard the bail amount. Then, I marched right up to Raul and demanded he make me full-time. I don't think he knew why I asked, or cared, just assumed I was desperate to save up for college.

I press the phone into my shoulder. "Ada, finish your applesauce, please. I'll be right back."

At the dining table, Ada nods. She moves her spoon as if it's heavy. Her face is the unusual one compared to her siblings. Jaydon's skin is deep brown, and when he stands in the sun he glows. Ada's skin is the color of sand, barely darkening at her forehead. Where his nose widens, hers turns up. The only thing similar is the brow. Heavy lids that blink only when they need to and eyelashes so long they curl into the eye, like yesterday; I held her while she cried and I flicked one out with my fingernail.

I step into my room and the door creaks when it closes.

"You know how old people have sets of fake teeth? Guess we'd have to get you some," he continues.

"Mmm. But would you still love me?"

"Yeah. What about you, would you love me?"

A pause. "Yes."

After that, it's silent for a while.

I run my tongue around my whole mouth. When I was younger, I feared that thinking or saying something over and over would make it come true. If I thought about the devil long enough, he would appear in my room. But none of us can ever predict reality. I couldn't have.

The prison ends the call abruptly as it often does, without even a chance for a goodby.

Thirty minutes later, I walk back to the kitchen and grab my lunch box. I peek at the inside and take out a half-eaten granola bar and crumpled napkins. A big stain ruins the bottom from my last day of school. Instead of eating at the cafeteria, all us seniors went to the McDonald's on the corner and signed each other's yearbooks with greasy French-fry fingers and hearts and promises to keep in touch. The full thermos of soup jostled around and spilled.

The refrigerator has leftovers neither me nor Mom want. It wasn't very good to begin with since I don't know how to cook. The microwave at work only functions at half power but it'll have to do today. I grab a baked chicken leg.

Behind the refrigerator door, Ada's bowl is empty and her spoon rests next to it, licked cleanly.

"Ada? Are you in the bathroom, sweetheart?" Silence. I zip up my lunch box.

"Ada?" The bathroom is empty. "I know you can hear me. Are we playing hide and seek?"

She's almost three but she doesn't say much. Definitely doesn't ask, "Why is the sky blue?" like what I read online that kids might start asking at this age. Maybe we both fear the day she does, since I won't know what to tell her, what would be appropriate to introduce.

"Oh! There you are."

She's standing in the doorway to my bedroom looking in. She could be looking at a number of things: my old pink dollhouse now crammed full of books, old knickknacks I can't let go of like a robotic dog that moves its head side to side when you press a button. She turns my way and widens her eyes.

Two weeks ago, the last time Jaydon was here, we watched a documentary. His surprise that he'd hinted at over text was a bag of microwavable popcorn with extra butter, two hot chocolate packets, and a movie he pirated. We lay perfectly still so my bed wouldn't creak and every few minutes switched who held the phone so our arms wouldn't hurt.

I want to study English in college, so the film was about linguists discussing the hardest and least spoken languages in the world. Jaydon fell asleep after thirty minutes, his breath sweet and salty and his head heavy on my shoulder. I was warm off the hot cocoa and with him and that slightly fuzzy film, I felt like I had everything.

One of the languages covered is spoken by the Pirahã people in Brazil. They don't have words for numbers, colors, or past or future tense. They don't understand abstract concepts like people leaving and if you can't see or physically observe something it doesn't exist.

Jaydon is Ada's favorite sibling and I keep waiting for her to throw a tantrum or ask where he is. Each time she bites her lip and furrows her brow in some kind of thought, I immediately prepare answers that she could understand—he went away for a while but he's going to come back. We're all working really hard on it. None of us like this arrangement any more than you do—but once she's done thinking all she does is blink. Like now, for her I didn't exist a few moments before. Every time I enter the room, she looks at me like I'm new.

Cynthia Roepke (aka Cynthia Breeding)

Cynthia Breeding often wonders if she was born in the wrong century. She is a well-established romance writer with over 50 novels and novellas available.

Cruising Along Nostalgia Road

Prologue

May, 1969

Trust Jack O'Neill to pull something off. At least, it wasn't his pants as he'd been threatening to moon the audience of proud parents, grandparents and dignitaries at the graduation of the Class of 1969.

Samantha—Sam—Olson shook her head as she pushed a stray curl back under her graduation cap. She doubted that the folks of Gainesbury, Texas, population 2,506, would ever have been the same if Jack had followed through with his antics. It was bad enough that he'd managed to conceal several frogs under his gown as they marched into the school auditorium. She'd seen him release them as they passed by the speaker's podium. It was only a matter of minutes before Mrs. Jones, the Baptist pastor's wife, would step forward to deliver the invocation and she'd totally freak-out.

Sam let her glance slip sideways as she took her seat on the makeshift bleachers that had been set on the stage. Jack was sitting in front and slightly to the right of her, looking angelic. Which, of course, was part of the problem. He *always* looked angelic with his mop of burnished gold hair that fell over his forehead and eyes as azure blue as the Texas sky. Most of the girls thought he was a real hunk. Coupled with an easy smile that showed a dimple in his left cheek and perfect manners whenever he was questioned, he never got blamed for anything. And *that* list was long…

As if he sensed her watching him, he turned his head and gave her his disarming smile. Except that she was not disarmed by it. Having lived next door to him for ten years, she'd witnessed far too many of his pranks and even been the victim of some, much to her chagrin. Now she narrowed her eyes at him, silently letting him know she'd seen the frogs. That only made him widen his grin and give her a wink before facing the front again.

It was a good thing they wouldn't be attending the same college in the fall.

The school band began the *Star Spangled Banner* and everyone rose as the ROTC color guard presented the flag. Mrs. Jones stepped to the podium as the anthem ended and, but a second later, emitted a shriek that rivaled any soprano hitting the high note of F in the "land of the free" line. Papers that had been placed on the podium so speakers wouldn't have to carry them went flying everywhere as Mrs Jones grabbed the stand in an attempt to levitate herself above the now-hopping frogs.

The audience sat in stunned silence as the class of 1969 tried not to titter, although a few laughed outright. Definitely not cool right now. The principal, Mr. Wilhelm—a man with the bearing of a general—glared at the class, in particular Jack, as he marched across the floor.

Jack wore a benign look as though he, too, was bewildered by the chaos.

Sam just hoped they would receive their diplomas this evening. Their principal, a direct descendent from German settlers who'd come to Texas in the 1800s, was not known for his sense of humor. She was pretty sure he didn't have one.

By this time, the pastor had gotten on the stage and was escorting his still nearly hysterical wife away. Father Hernandez, priest of the local parish, stepped forward to take her place, but he, too, paused to look at Jack. Sam recalled that the kindly priest had attempted to make Jack an altar boy at one time. His stint was short-lived, although she never found out why.

It took several more minutes to corral the frogs and Sam glanced at Jack again, wondering if he had any other surprises for tonight. Once more, he caught her eye. She frowned at him, but he just smiled. An infuriatingly innocent-looking smile.

Thankfully, he had not further pranks planned—or maybe he actually wanted to receive his diploma—and the rest of the ceremony went smoothly.

Sam sighed in relief as their names were read and they proceeded across the stage. Perhaps the earlier chaos that Jack had created had been somewhat symbolic of their past years. They'd witnessed several assassinations, along with anti-war protests and Civil Rights riots. Perhaps, like the second half of this evening, now things would begin to smooth out.

The band played the school's fight song and, as they filed out, the choir began to sing the 5th Dimension's *Age of Aquarius*.

When the moon is in the 7th house
And Jupiter aligns with Mars
Then peace will guide the planets
And love will steer the stars...

Soon it would be the beginning of a new decade for the Graduating Class of 1969

David Carpenter

My name is David Carpenter: Writer of stories, adopter of cats, player of games. Graduate of the United States Coast Guard Academy with a second degree from the university formerly known as Corpus Christi State. After a stint in the Coast Guard, I became a computer programmer, a choice that I enjoyed but would not recommend for normal people. I live in Corpus Christi, Texas and write urban fantasy with a touch of humor.

Big Dwayne Harris

Dwayne Harris swung the heavy, six-bar bull gate closed behind his truck. As the local game warden, he didn't need to ask permission. But as a one-time ranch hand, he considered it a distinct privilege to be allowed to pass through another man's gate. There was a kind of a mystical aspect to it, a recognition that gates mark boundaries, boundaries that should only be crossed with prudence and respect.

That was especially true here on the Tres Colinas Ranch, a high-desert grassland that flowed gently up to rugged, rock-strewn mountains that rose from the desert floor like islands rising from the sea. It looked desolate, but there was all manner of game here: mule deer and antelope, turkey and quail, along with more exotic animals, like bighorn sheep. The terrain could be deceptive—the open, rolling plain concealed a complex network of gullies, dry creeks and arroyos that had been carved by centuries of late-summer rains.

You could hide almost anything in some of those arroyos.

Dwayne slid back into the driver's seat, his breath condensing in the cold, dry air. It was still dark, but there was a faint line of red on the eastern horizon. This section of the Tres Colinas was one of the more remote areas butting up against the Sierra Diablo: thirty miles off the highway, plus another hundred to the nearest town. Most poachers knew better than to trespass here, but the lure of bagging an exotic sometimes attracted a darker, more dangerous breed.

His quarry would be just ahead, waiting for daylight. It was an odd time of year for hunters, and odder yet that Felipe Mondragon would give anyone permission to hunt his fifty-thousand-acre spread. The old man fiercely guarded his privacy— even the Feds had to get special permission to enter the property. Legend had it that Felipe once chased a Shell Oil geologist off the ranch with a shotgun.

There was, however, one exception to the rule. The local game warden had unfettered access, based on a century-old arrangement between the Mondragon family and the State of Texas. That warden was hand-picked by Colonel Masterson, Director of Law Enforcement for Texas Parks and Wildlife, and personally approved by Felipe Mondragon. It was a one-of-a-kind appointment, complete with lifetime tenure and a whale of a non-disclosure agreement.

There were a lot of tall tales surrounding the Tres Colinas, ghost stories of hunters who went out and never came back. Hunters who weren't prepared for some of the weirder things that could be found in the foothills of the Sierra Diablo. *Bestias Monstruos*, the old-timers called them.

Once, back in the 1980's, some trophy hunter from Boston offered a much younger Felipe Mondragon a suitcase full of money for an unsupervised hunt. They found the trophy hunter's empty truck a few days later. The game warden, half a dozen ranch hands and a DPS helicopter scoured the area for a week, but the man's remains were never found.

Dwayne wasn't about to let something like *that* happen again.

He put the big Chevy Silverado into gear and eased on down the rocky, unimproved road, driving slow with the headlights off. After about three miles, he stopped in a low spot and shut down the engine. Like all game wardens, Dwayne preferred to maintain an element of surprise. You could tell a lot about a man's intentions by how he reacted when a lawman popped up out of nowhere.

The three out-of-staters were standing around their rented Nissan crew cab, facing the sunrise, hands shoved in the pockets of their jeans to ward off the cold. None of them were looking his way. He glided silently around a patch of creosote bushes and approached them from behind.

"How you boys doin' this mornin'?"

Dwayne's voice was a basso rumble that climbed up to a pleasant East Texas drawl, and the unexpected sound made all three men jump.

The closest exhaled loudly and exclaimed, "What the hell, mate?"

"Crikey, he's a big un', ini' he?"

"Quiet, you twits. That's *him*. The one the clerk told us about. Big Dwayne, the game warden."

Young, fit, and British. That's how Molly described them. She ran the Day's Inn in Van Horn, and had tipped Dwayne off about three strange young men who were talking about hunting the Tres Colinas. There was something about these boys—he couldn't bring himself to think of them as men, despite the muscles bulging beneath the flannel shirts— that set his instincts buzzing. Young bucks, looking to make their mark. He had seen their kind before, but it had been years since any had ventured into his jurisdiction. Old Man Mondragon had a soft spot for the old days, and if Dwayne's hunch was right, these young men would be about as old-fashioned as you could get. It was the kind of thing that might make it hard for Felipe to say no.

Dwayne kept a professional smile on his face and an easy-going tone in his voice. Nearly everyone in the county referred to him as 'Big' Dwayne, although most were too polite to say it to his face. At six foot six, he towered over the trio of young, athletic-looking Brits.

"Texas game warden, gentlemen. Would you mind showing me your licenses and ID's?"

They shuffled around, rummaging in a leather satchel that contained their money and documents. Molly claimed that all they had were long guns, but Dwayne kept an eye on their hands anyway, using a flashlight in the pale pre-dawn light. They presented passports instead of driver's licenses, but everything was in order.

"What you boys gunnin' for today?"

"Scaled quail." The tallest of the three grinned up at him, trying to look confident. His passport listed him as James McAvoy. His friends were William Butler and Allan Cumming. All three had just turned eighteen years of age.

"Blues, huh? A little off the beaten track, if you don't mind my sayin'. But you're likely to find some, down in that arroyo."

Butler and Cumming exchanged a furtive glance at the word 'Blues'.

McAvoy flashed a guileless smile. "My thoughts exactly, officer. Would you mind if I asked, sir, how you knew to look for us here? We were under the impression that this is private property."

"Word gets around, you know how it is. And you're right about it being private property. I'm going to need to see your letter."

"Oh, you mean from Mr. Mondragon? Of course."

McAvoy pulled a folded piece of paper from his shirt pocket and handed it over.

Dwayne read it briefly and handed it back. "It doesn't specify quail. In fact, it doesn't say anything about what you're huntin' today."

"Oh. Is that a problem?"

"No, not if all you're gonna to do is shoot a few quail. I'm going to need to take a look at your guns. Are they in the truck, there?"

McAvoy moved quickly towards the truck. "No, sir, we've got them here, in the bed. I'll hand them down to you." He dropped the tailgate, revealing three shotguns. He handled the weapons with care, opening the action before handing each one over, making sure he kept the muzzle pointed in a safe direction. Young Mr. McAvoy was no stranger to firearms.

The guns were all brand-new, TriStar Hunter EX's, a cheap over-under sold by Wal-Mart. None of them were loaded.

"These guns belong to you?"

McAvoy held up a wrinkled receipt. "Yes, sir. We purchased them in Del Rio."

"Uh-huh. Let's have a look at your ammunition."

Mister Cumming hauled out a crate with half a dozen boxes of shotgun shells inside. "Here, sir. Do you want me to open one up?"

Dwayne checked the label and shook his head. "Nope, these are fine."

There were three lariats lying in big coils near the back of the truck bed. A pretty common sight in ranch country, but these boys weren't cowhands. And lariats didn't usually have hooked chains in place of a loop.

"Everything all right, officer?"

"Yup, you're good to go for your quail hunt. Just one thing, though—I'm gonna need to take a look inside that truck."

Any doubts Dwayne might have had were instantly banished by the look on McAvoy's face.

"Ah, inside the truck, sir? Well, ah, I--"

The tow-headed one, the one named Butler, stepped off to the side and pulled a small stick from his sleeve. He pointed it at Dwayne and began muttering in what sounded like Latin.

Dwayne covered the distance in one long, sudden stride and dropped a hand the size of a shovel on Butler's shoulder. Butler stared up at him in wide-eyed amazement, his weird chant frozen in mid-word.

"Mr. Butler, I'm gonna have to ask you to stop doin' that."

He snatched the stick out of the young man's hand as easily as he might have taken it from a child, tucking it into his belt with one quick, efficient motion. Butler tried to twist away and gasped in pain as the warden clamped down on his shoulder. Dwayne's other hand moved to the butt of his sidearm. "You boys step over there where I can keep an eye on you. You too, Mister Butler. And keep your hands where I can see them. "

Dwayne had a pretty good idea what he was dealing with now, sure enough to forgo cuffing and frisking them. These young gentlemen weren't used to being recognized; Butler had assumed he could finesse the situation. But they weren't likely to try anything serious— Virtue, Chivalry, and Service was their motto. Or soon would be if they managed to pass their test.

McAvoy tried to smooth things over.

"Sir, I apologize for this unfortunate misunderstanding--"

Dwayne cut him off.

"Interferin' with a law officer is a serious offense, gentlemen. Am I makin' myself clear?"

They nodded glumly as he opened the door and began rummaging around on the back seat. He grunted and pulled out a sheathed long sword.

"Who does this belong to?"

Allan Cumming raised a hesitant hand.

"Vorpal blades are not allowed in the Sierra Diablo, Mister Cumming. I'm afraid I'm gonna have to confiscate it, along with Mr.

Butler's wand. I'll write you out a receipt, and you can take it up with Judge DeLeon if you feel like contesting it." He waved a hand at the truck. "The enchanted crossbow is a gray area, but according to the Scottish Addenda of 1840, that's at *my* discretion, and I'm gonna allow it. The rest of it's fine, although your chain mail is a little on the puny side, if you don't mind my sayin'."

McAvoy and his companions gaped at him and then at each other. "You know what a Vorpal Blade is?"

"I guess you could say I know a thing or two about the Order of Saint George. Been a while, though. You boys part of a new crop of Initiates? Uh-huh, thought so. All right, I'm going to need to see your huntin' license. The *other* one."

The three Initiates exchanged glances, then McAvoy fetched the leather satchel. Inside was a small piece of rolled parchment, covered in sigils and signed with a wax seal.

Dwayne examined it carefully, nodded, and handed it back. These boys were green, but they had a valid license, and Felipe had given his permission. And the Order wouldn't have sent them here if they weren't ready.

"All right, gentlemen. This license is good for catch-and-release only, and that means no souvenirs, not even a claw or a scale. Just so you know, I'll be keepin' an eye on you, and Judge DeLeon goes pretty hard on that sort of thing. Mister Butler—"

"Sir?" Butler was trying to take it like a man, but he couldn't keep a faint quaver out of his voice.

"I'd be within my rights to arrest you for assault on a law officer. It doesn't matter one bit that it was just a Spell of Lesser Deceit."

Butler looked sad. "Yes, sir."

"But if I arrested every two-bit yahoo who tried to lie to me, Judge DeLeon would run out of space in his jail. So I'm gonna let it go, this time. But you can pretty much kiss that wand of yours goodbye. Are we clear? Good."

Dwayne tucked the longsword under his arm and wrote them a receipt for their confiscated property, along with a warning citation for William Butler.

"Now listen up. You want to hunt rock dragons, you've come to the right place. They're ambush predators and are well-nigh impossible to spot in some of these stone formations, so keep your eyes open and your wits about you. If you do manage to find one it pays to remember that they have a *real* short temper. A typical specimen in the Sierra Diablo will weigh in at around twelve hundred pounds, and their scales will turn anything from a longsword to a thirty-ought-six, but they *will* go down if you can clap 'em on the back of the head hard enough. You can expect to get roughed up some, there's a pretty good emergency clinic in Van Horn, if it comes to that. But-- "He pointed his index finger at them "-- if you see something with a blue frill, you turn around and go the other way. You hear me?" The big man chuckled. "You mess with Old Blue and he'll eat the three of you for breakfast. Chain mail and all."

He left them gaping open-mouthed as he strode back into the brush, maintaining the illusion that on the Tres Colinas, a Texas Game Warden can appear anywhere, at any time, from any direction.

Especially when that Game Warden happens to be Big Dwayne Harris.

Devorah Fox

"What if?" Those two words all too easily send Devorah Fox spinning into flights of fancy. She writes mysteries, fantasies, and thrillers, and is the author of 50 books and short stories.

The Closer © 2022

He was going to have to kill her. He didn't know her name, where she came from, what she did, what she was doing in this hotel, or even what she looked like, although he could imagine. A big woman. Puffy face. Piggy eyes. Thin bleached-out hair. Of course, she might not look like that at all. He didn't know; he hadn't seen her yet. It didn't matter. None of it—her appearance, her occupation, her reason for being in the room next to his—had anything to do with why he had to kill her.

He lay on the hotel bed and stared. Room-darkening drapes produced a dense blackness against which he could project the pictures he saw in his mind. He had never killed anyone before—or should he say yet, since it seemed he would have to kill her. But he didn't doubt he could. He achieved every goal he or anyone else set for him. He had earned his moniker, The Closer.

How would he do it? Shoot her? No, too noisy. And—admit it, he told himself—too quick. Yes, he wanted her to suffer as he had suffered. So, poison? Too remote, too impersonal. He wanted her to know as she died who was the agent of her death. He wanted to see her pupils widen with comprehension before death turned her eyes to glass. Strangling, then?

The Closer imagined his hands around her throat. A fat woman like her, the neck would be fleshy and thick. He would have to squeeze until his fingertips went white and his wrists ached. Would she make a noise? How would that sound? Like the throttled gurgling she made now, as she lay snoring in the room next door, unaware of his growing fury?

Stab her, then. Or cut her cursed blubbery throat. There'd be no noise that way.

Long into the night, The Closer lay awake entertaining himself with such fantasies, while under the surface his rage festered.

###

It seemed he had gotten to sleep only minutes ago when the wake-up call roused him. He might as well not have slept for all the good it did him. He hated having to face the day not well-rested. Lack of sleep slowed his reactions and thought processes. It wouldn't jeopardize his success. He would prevail despite his fatigue but it would make his work harder. Damn her for keeping him awake!

He picked up the attaché case, left his room, and called the elevator. No sooner had a bell chimed to signal its arrival, the door of the room next to his opened. She stepped out, the woman who had robbed him of his sleep, stolen his night.

"Oh, hold that, please," she called, and hurried to join him in the tall, narrow car.

She was not fat and piggy-faced. Instead, she was petite with sleekly-styled hair. Her pink lips smiled at him, albeit tentatively, and almond-shaped brown eyes, though friendly, betrayed a hint of unease. She gripped the handle of her purse with both hands, and he wondered if she had perceived his enmity. It had been strong enough to penetrate the thin wall separating their rooms.

Under other circumstances, he would have made a play for her, although a woman as attractive as she was unlikely to go for someone like him. He bore no illusions about his homeliness: medium build, thin brown hair, brown eyes in an almost soft, clean-shaven face. Nor did he resent it. His unspectacular looks aided him in his work.

He strode to the front desk. Out of the corner of his eye, he watched her exit the hotel. The draft from the rotating door fluttered the skirt of her silky dress. He turned to the front desk man and asked, "The lady in 410, is she staying another night?"

The clerk smiled and nodded. "She booked it for a week, Romeo."

She may have, The Closer thought. Nevertheless, tomorrow someone else would occupy Room 410.

It was late evening when The Closer stepped from the elevator into the fourth-floor corridor. Once again, he had proved he was aptly named, though it had cost him a long day with no time to stop even for meals. He'd been too busy to give the woman in 410 a moment's thought, but as he passed her door he tensed. His brain flooded with the images he had conjured last night. Before this night was over, he would take action. First, he absolutely had to get some sleep.

###

The scream was unlike anything he had heard before, the last desperate cry of a helpless animal facing its inescapable extermination. The wailing went on long past the moment it yanked him upright in his bed, continued uninterrupted as he sprinted from his room. Hair standing on end from the sheer terror in the scream, he pounded on the door to Room 410.

"Miss, are you all right?" he called. No response. He rattled the doorknob. Locked! He hurled himself at the wooden panel. It wouldn't budge, and still, she screamed. Aiming his shoulder at the door, he rammed it with a strength he didn't know he possessed. The wood cracked. He flung the shards aside and stepped through. Moonlight from the uncurtained window spotlighted her where she lay in bed, screaming still. He raced to her.

"Miss! Miss!" He clasped her shoulders and shook her.

Her eyes opened. She stared at him unseeing, but the scream did stop. Several minutes passed while she gasped for breath and her eyes lost their unfocused look. "Oh, it's you. I, I—"

"What was it?" The Closer asked. "A nightmare?"

She shook her tousled head. "More like night terrors. I dreamed I was being slashed."

The Closer felt his face grow warm with embarrassment as he remembered his murderous fantasy from last night. From what dark corner of his soul had those vivid homicidal visions come?

"It went on and on, I was powerless to escape." She took several deep breaths. "I guess I'm worried about going 'under the knife.' I'm having surgery tomorrow. For sleep apnea. It gives me the most awful snoring." Her eyelids lowered. "Perhaps you heard me. I know it can get very loud."

"Yes, I heard you," he replied. "Kept me up all last night. I thought if it continued another night I was going to have to kill you." He chuckled. "Or at least get you to change rooms. I'm a traveling salesman, I need my sleep."

"Oh, I'm so sorry," she said. "I will switch rooms if you like. But I hope to be getting better. I'm in town to see an otolaryngologist, an ear-nose-and-throat specialist. He'll perform an operation that should help."

"I'm sure everything will go just fine. Don't worry," said The Closer.

"Thanks for the vote of confidence," she replied. "Again, I apologize. I will change rooms. Right now." She reached for the bedside phone.

He caught her still trembling hand. "Oh no, you don't. I wouldn't be able to keep tabs on you that way."

She dipped her head. When she raised it, her eyes were bright and merry. "You're an angel. How can I ever repay you?"

"Have dinner with me? As soon as you recuperate? I'll be in town all week."

"I'd like nothing better," she replied.

"You've got it, Pretty Lady." He smiled. Another deal consummated. Yessir, they didn't call him The Closer for nothing.

—End—

Donna Huddleston

Before her retirement, Dr. Donna Huddleston served at Del Mar College as a nurse educator in the Department of Nursing Education. Currently, she is the Accredited Provider Program Director at Del Mar College, Department of Continuing Education.

Destination Boquillas, Mexico

The Chihuahua Desert and the Sierra del Carmen Mountain range straddle the Rio Grande River in Southwest Texas. Surreal scenery abounds. We drove past miles of short palm-looking yucca and agave with their tall plumes dotting the desert as we made our way to the Big Bend National Park and across the river to Boquillas, Mexico. Roadrunners darted across the road. A lone coyote slunk into the vegetation along the side of the road where small-sized white-tailed deer munched on the grass.

On the way there, at an abandoned rest stop on the side of the road, a placard told the story of a pioneer woman, Nina Hannold. She moved to the Texas desert in 1908 to homestead with her husband, Curtis Lloyd. Under the shade of cottonwood trees near a spring that she loved, she read to her stepchildren. Both the cottonwoods and the spring are long gone due to climate change. Nina's grave remains. She died of uremic poisoning, a blood disorder resulting from kidney failure during pregnancy.

We finally reached the U.S. immigration building. People describe me as adventuresome. I agree. Nevertheless, I'm just over 70 and overweight. My husband is in his late 80's and at times, wobbly. I asked the ranger on duty. "Do you think crossing the river is hazardous?"

"No, you should be fine," he said. "Just read the sign outside the building and follow the instructions. Remember most people don't speak English."

We hiked down the short path to the water's edge. To get to the other side, we had three choices: find a narrow part to wade across, swim, or take a rowboat. The day we went, two rowboats were ferrying tourists across the river. We took the rowboat for $5.00 each roundtrip.

Once across the river, more transportation choices awaited us to reach the village. There was a horse, a donkey or burro, or a truck. Walking was not recommended as the road is ungraded, hot and dusty. We picked a 2001 F150 truck with a driver named Omar who charged us

$10.00 each, roundtrip and he included a tour of the village. The first place we passed was his home where Veronica his wife was hanging embroidered crafts with themes of roosters and rabbits on their fence. On the way back, we asked him to stop and we purchased five of them for $10.00 each.

In the meantime, my husband, Lee and I shared a traditional Mexican lunch. Mounds of beef tacos, chips and salsa, Spanish rice, and refried beans covered the colorful plates. Topo Chico, sparkling water quenched our thirst and helped wash down the huge servings of food. We ate outside on a covered porch overlooking the canyon at *Jose Falcon*'s one of the two restaurants in the village. The other restaurant is across the street. Our driver, Omar then took us on a tour of the village and showed us the newly installed solar panels, a gift from the Mexican government. A Catholic chapel, another church, a clinic, and a school were interspersed among colorfully painted adobe-like homes.

After the lunch, the tour, and the stop to purchase Veronica's embroidery, we bounced in Omar's truck along the banks of the river before returning to the United States. There was no pier for the boat. This time we went in a different rowboat with a different skipper.

The skipper was an older, wiry man who guided us down the bank; the bank was steeper on this side. My husband and I were unsteady on the rough terrain. The skipper was strong. He helped me step down the dirt embankment, and board the rowboat even though I felt like I might fall face forward. He pointed to the prow of the boat, nodded for me to walk along the bottom of the boat, and then step over the thwart where he would sit to row.

Clumsily, I did just that. "Do you want me to row?" I asked, jokingly. My husband was already seated in the stern.

"Do you want me to give the boat a shove and it will take you to the Gulf?" the man said. He could speak English! He grinned but I was not sure that somewhere underneath, he really meant it.

I looked up into his brown eyes lined with wrinkles. He had one foot one on the bank and the other in the boat. We were about the same age. The resentment was palpable. I could traverse this river so freely and enter both countries unimpeded by immigration. "No, I want you to take us across." I felt humbled by him and this experience.

On the return to the U.S. and after inserting our passports into a machine for reentry, a four-year-old stood sobbing on the veranda of the immigration building. "What is the matter," I asked her mother.

"She is crying because her donkey was too slow." Immediately, pictures of the child riding on a fast donkey, her brown hair flowing behind her, and her heels kicking to go even faster across the desert filled my mind. I wouldn't mind that; what fun!

Donna Lea Anderson

Donna Lea Anderson has written two novels. *The Adventurous Three* is a well-received children's book illustrated with her own drawings. It follows Hummie the Hummingbird, Sammie the crawfish, and Attie the mockingbird. *Unforeseen Predator* is a much different novel. In this excerpt, Charmaine hopes for a fresh start in Corpus Christi, Texas.

An excerpt from ***Unforeseen Predator***

Within days Charmaine rents a cheap garage apartment located near six points (six roads that inter meet at one intersection). It's not the Taj Mahal but compared to what she was raised in, it feels and looks like it. Lucky for Charmaine the apartment is furnished with a small television and phone. It is also within walking distance to her new job waiting tables at Shepp's Diner, a twenty-four-hour diner located in the six point's area. The pay isn't great which means she will have to rely on tips to help pay the bills.

It doesn't take Charmaine long to fall in love with Corpus Christi and her new surroundings. Her weary, damaged soul finds comfort with the towns swaying palm trees, sea gulls, and thick, salty breezes blowing off the bay. Her walk to and from work isn't too bad but waiting tables and standing on her feet for eight hours or more isn't easy. As tough as life is, when it comes to Charmaine, she never complains even though her feet hurt and back aches continuously. She looks at it this way: no need to complain, a girl's got to do what she's got to do to make money, and in a lawful way. Even though money is tight, she strives forward, works hard, wasting none, and saves every little extra nickel and dime that comes her way.

Immediately, Charmaine becomes a model employee at work, and though the job has its disadvantages, it keeps her lawful and off the streets and from returning to prostitution. After being raised as a prostitute and held hostage for her entire life the opportunity and desire to let her light shine and be a good example for others is extremely important, she desires and is ready for the Christian lifestyle which she was always denied.

Although a model employee she now has a few personal issues to deal with. She quickly learns that life outside of Little Wicked can also be just as tough, as her shyness and being an introvert stands in her way of mingling and befriending others. So, as the new employee and, as she struggles with her inner demons, she finds that most at work are friendly, and even her Boss comes across as a perfect gentleman, treating women with respect. For Charmaine this will take some getting used to, since she's never been around men who act and show their gentlemen side.

Dylan Lopez

Dylan Lopez is a senior at Texas A&M University-Corpus Christi pursuing a degree in English. A student of Joseph Wilson and Tom Murphy, he is currently the Managing Editor for The Windward Review.

Ode to my Journal

To my white-worn journal,
with pressed pages,
severe, and empty.
A hardcover desert,
hot edges defined by
indelible blankness.

You are my future unwritten,
the novella of my near tomorrows
and offshore years unexplored.

I will write you, someday.
Sear your silver sheets
with cloudy pigments—
my unfolded daydreams
and songs half-sung,
My life, laid bare.

Introduction to Poetry

A poem begins as a speck of dust,
held captive in the soft light
of a waiting world

or set free, loosed on scarlet lips.

Sometimes a poem sinks,
deep into the flood waters
lost in a forest of mud-caked reeds.

I reach beneath the surface,
and grasp the nameless corpse.

I want them to float
like gilded gondoliers
embroidered with dark pigments
across their blank skin.

But they visit me in the quiet dark
with their own revisions.
They smother my gentle dreams
in the crib, cooing farewell.

They take turns with the carving knife,
they pierce my paper skin—

They let the light in.

D Weiss

D. Weiss was born and raised in Corpus Christi. She is an English major at Texas A&M CC. She has been writing practically since she learned how to read. Her biggest writing influences are James Patterson and Maya Angelou. She's also a traditional and digital artist, and is currently working on a light novel. One of her favorite pastimes is playing D&D.

A Meeting with the Fae

I once had a meeting with the Fae.
Seeking answers to questions long pondered, I wished to settle the matter for good.
Just how accepting is the Fae of a new companion in their vast woods?
Is it really spiriting away if one chooses to leave?

If they prove kind, whether they stand big or small, it would be a joy to dance in their enchanted halls.
Ah, how freeing the notion is to dance without care for the world left behind,
To dance lacking a single treacherous thought in one's mind.

I once had a meeting with the Fae.
A meek human, unassuming and plain, with more to lose rather than gain.
With a nod and a smile, I was ushered to a toadstool table,
Surrounded by seats of pine, though of course,
I could not allow myself to partake of a morsel or drop of wine.
How easy it would have been in the presence of such beauty to sit and stare,
Yet, I resolved to keep my intentions bare.

My real name I held close to my chest, tales of Fae being those I knew best.
Gods forgive me, a moment of weakness I did have to quell,
For though the Fae were strangers, how they seemed to know me so well.
While the Fae were crafty and a slip of the tongue could seal my fate,
They were perhaps the most honest people I had met to date.

Eyes shining with mischief and allure, I did not shrink under their gaze.
In a clearing among actors, I proved an impostor no longer.
However, soon came the time for our rendezvous to end,
And I was allowed to hop the circle back to my house around the bend.

I once had a meeting with the Fae.
Occasionally, I hear their voices on the wind,
And I am brought back to that day. They call me,
Offering a chance to right the choice they recall as my sole error,
"Return to us and stay."

Elizabeth N. Flores

Elizabeth N. Flores taught government/political science for 43 years at Del Mar College and was the college's first Mexican American Studies Program Coordinator. Flores earned an MA in Political Science at the University of Michigan and a BA in Political Science at St. Mary's University. She was awarded the LULAC Council 1 Educator of the Year Award (2014) and the Del Mar College Dr. Aileen Creighton Award for Teaching Excellence (2013). Flores retired from teaching in 2022. Writing poetry about family, memory and culture is her current area of interest.

Tribute

I wish I knew the boy's name.
He paid tribute to my dad,
a man I'm sure he didn't know,
as we left St. Joseph's Church on
19th Street and headed to Holy Cross Cemetery.

The boy looked about ten.
He was sitting on the porch of a
house that also served as a
beauty shop for this
Westside neighborhood
and former neighbors
who now lived far and wide
on Corpus Christi's Southside.

He was playing checkers
with an old man, probably his grandpa.

The boy looked up from the checkerboard
as our funeral procession passed, removed
his baseball cap, and ever so slightly
bowed his head.

I think back to the rituals at the church and the
cemetery that helped us pay tribute to a man
whose life was full and heart so big.

The little boy who effortlessly lay his head bare with
a willful nod brought the most comfort to my sad heart.

In my mind he joined the procession, and his presence
gave me the resolve to keep going, follow the road,
stay on 19th Street until we reached
that place where we lay the man down
to enjoy his final peaceful rest.

Emma Helene Guerra

Emma Helene Guerra is a recent graduate from Texas A&M University – Corpus Christi as well as a current graduate student at the University of Texas – Rio Grande Valley. With a strong passion for LGBTQ+, mental health, and women's issues, most of her work reflects a balance of all three of these factors when developing her own identity in a world that is constantly in motion.

Tooth Decay

I can feel my teeth rotting inside my mouth.
Brown-grey cavities jutting out in mangled bone
piercing my gums.

My tongue licking up the bitter taste of blood mixed
with saliva, my spit turning a burnt orange against the
porcelain sinkstained with mold and hair dye in shades
of black and blue.
A bruise on the delicate skin of emotional stability.

I remember how jealous I was of my younger
brother who left each dentist appointment with a
clean record, not racking up hefty bills for
pulled teeth and silver molars. His brush
remaining dry. Nightmares consumed my mind
of each delicate tooth falling from its spot,
my tiny pink hands unable to hold it all.
Every word equaled another sacrifice
as I pay close attention to not swallow one,
it would cut up my insides and I would simply
die. Soon enough, the pile would overflow
falling
down
slowly

into the black void of no return

I

wanted

help

from the thoughts I could not control, and the harm being inflicted upon myself. All by myself, but I did not want to die. Letting go was not an option like the strangers online told me it was. Despite the warning sign, physical and verbal, my issues often went ignored and forgotten. Brushed under the tethered rug of academic achievement. Perfection was the unsaid bar I had expected myself to reach, a bar that a child's hands cannot touch. My brother did not feel the need to reach that same height. I wonder if my parents just heard his screams better since they did not sound like mine.

I remember how jealous I was of my younger brother.

Gerald Beckman

Gerald Beckman was born and raised on a farm in West Texas and practiced law in Corpus Christi for many years. Since retirement, he has written several novels. These include *The Family*, *When Latin Lost Its Relevance*, *Roughnecks and Rednecks*, and *Powder Road*. His work is intensely evocative of all things Texas—whether it's West Texas or South Texas. Recently, he's taken up oil painting, often choosing the rugged, West Texas terrain as a subject.

An excerpt from ***When Latin Lost Ists Relevance***

The next morning after Mass and a breakfast of cold cereal eaten in silence, we reported for Latin class at eight o'clock. Only the sextaners had to be in their classroom at 7:55 and I was now a quintaner. Already I was seeing the advantages of class preference.

And sure enough, everybody was there before the bell shattered the air at exactly eight o'clock. A short, moonfaced young priest breezed into the classroom, head down, left arm swinging, right arm loaded with books, tablets and a manila folder. His name was Father James, but his head was as round and bald as a light bulb. "Chromedome" was a perfect fit. He tossed the materials on his desk, turned to the crucifix hanging on the wall at the front of the room, and after a hurried Sign of the Cross led the class in a quick version of the Hail Mary.

His back was to us during the prayer, so when Chuck saw me, he mouthed his astonishment, saying, I think, "What the hell you doing here?"

I was mouthing an answer when the prayer ended. Chromedome turned around and caught me. "Mr…?" Eyes wide open, brow furrowed, he was looking straight at me. By now we were all seated.

"Riddle, Father. Paul Riddle…"

"Mr. Riddle." He referred to a list. "I see you're new here – passed the placement test. A little weak in Latin, but…well, congratulations."

His eyebrows were still arched, even though he was looking down at the list. I could tell he had the same thoughts about what was in store for me as Father Marzen did, but he had the grace not to voice them. Not right then.

"Now I don't want to embarrass you Mr. Riddle," by now his eyebrows had reached the middle of his forehead, "but we have our own way of doing things here. For instance, while praying we pay attention to the prayers. We don't mug, wink, signal, wave, clap our hands, or whisper. Okay?" His eyebrows shot up even higher, pressing the wrinkles above them tighter together, but now there was a grin on his face – the same kind of grin Father Marzen had when he wished me luck. He held the pose for a long moment. I said nothing. For a guy not wanting to embarrass me, he sure seemed to enjoy doing it.

"Okay?" He said again, leaning farther forward.

"Oh – oh, yeah," I said.

Another line of furrows appeared above those already there. This guy had a world-class set of wrinkles on his forehead, I can tell you that. He was still on point, holding his pose like a well-trained retriever. I thought he was going to fall over frontward.

"I mean, yes – yes Father."

"Good." He relaxed and straightened up.

"Now tell me – where does a young man from a place called Far Corners Texas go to study Latin before he gets to high school?"

Everybody but me was getting a huge kick out of what was going on.

"I, uh, I – I didn't really study it, sir – Father, I mean. Sister Martina taught me some after school, sorta like for extra credit, you know, while I waited for my ride home – you know, from school."

"How remarkable. A natural Latin scholar."

"She taught all us servers Latin – you know, to serve Mass, after school. My ride was always late, and she knew I was going to the seminary, so I guess she thought…"

"Am I to understand a nun tutored you in Latin because you told her you were going to the seminary?"

My scalp started itching like crazy again. It always itched when I was embarrassed. "I dunno – I guess – she thought it would help, I guess, an' Dad let me stay after school to do it."

"He *let* you? Your father *let* you stay after school to study Latin? You *wanted* to study Latin?" Phony amazement was all over his face.

I didn't know what he was getting at. The other guys were grinning, some giggling. "Well, uh, yeah."

"You may be the first and only boy in history to volunteer to study Latin, and agree to stay after school to do it." He stopped, acting mystified, like he needed time to savor such a wondrous fact. I thought he was waiting for me to explain. I was so embarrassed I thought I'd start sweating blood in another minute. "Well," I finally blurted "it's more fun than hauling water to the chickens!"

Everybody howled at that. Chromedome enjoyed it as much as anybody, but he must have seen how miserable I was. He quieted the class and directed the discussion into a slightly different direction. "Yes, well, I suspect we're a little ahead of you in view of your score on the placement test. You'll have some serious catching up to do." He stared at me. "You didn't get any help when you took the test, did you?"

I stared back. A lie – I had to lie! "Well, no – 'course not, I mean – no, nobody helped me…" I had to protect Sister Martina, didn't I?

Then for the first time I saw a glimmer of what might have been genuine kindness on his face. I'm not sure he believed me a hundred percent, but he didn't make an issue of it. "I'll help you," he said suddenly. "I can't cut you any slack on assignments or tests, you understand, but anybody who bites off a chunk like you have – if you're willing to work at it, I'll spend extra time with you. And I'll ask Fr. Schmakel if he'd be willing to spend a little time with you too. You're going to need it."

Those words again.

"Fr. Schmakel is a brilliant man," he continued. "Brilliant. And sometimes he'll take on a deserving student, give him special help. Between the two of us we might be able to get you through. But you're going to have to work."

He stared at me like he expected me to say something, but my tongue was in a knot.

"I'll ask him if he'd be interested, but I have to warn you. He'll only help you if you convince him you're doing your best. Otherwise, he'll not waste his time. Understand?"

I nodded.

Then he called out Billy Childress's name. No frowning there, just a simple welcome to the class and a comment on how well he did on the placement test. The contrast was pretty awesome, and wasn't lost on anybody.

Class ended at 8:55 and geometry began at nine o'clock. A fifteen-minute recess followed at 9:55, then German at 10:10 and English at 11:05. At the noon bell a disembodied voice led the Angelus over the intercom, then we assembled in the hallway outside the study hall for the two-by-two march to the refectory. In silence. Always in silence.

Herb Canales

Spanish Jews fleeing the Inquisition arrived in New Spain as early as the 16th century. They settled in Monterrey and other areas and were the ancestors of many South Texas families. Herb Canales, a former Director of the Corpus Christi Library System, is researching this.history.

My Journey to Find My Roots

My interest in family history placed itself within historical context to create a broad narrative when I was in high school. My mother one day commented that a lady at work would go to La Retama Library in Corpus Christi at lunch time to work on her family tree.

I found that fascinating and wanted to do the same. So, one summer day, with time on my hands, I boarded a bus at Louisiana Avenue and Alameda and headed down to the library. Arriving in the Local History room I located just one relevant book – "The Romance of Spanish Surnames," by Charles Maduell. That was it. The rest of the genealogy collection consisted of works of Southern ancestry and English heritage. Understandably so, as the library depended largely on donations for its genealogical collection.

Also, as I would find out later, works on Hispanic genealogy were literally few and far between. The research and publishing boom had not begun, the Internet was decades away, and what little that had been published in Mexico was difficult to acquire.

The next point of inspiration was the series "Roots" which ran on the ABC television network in 1977. This chronicled the slave, Kunta Kinte. And his family. Still, it would be years before I would be able to do advanced research. In 1985 when Corpus Christi City Manager Ed Martin appointed me as director of the Corpus Christi Public Libraries, research opportunities began to present themselves. I enlisted the support of Dr. Clotilde P. Garcia, otherwise known as Dr. Cleo. She provided financial support which helped acquire a growing body of work. Dr. Cleo also funded the computerization of 18th and 19th century records from early border settlements in New Spain (Nueva España) to the frontier at or near the Rio Grande. This is where many South Texas Hispanic families originated.

History is not straightforward. It can be inspiring, fascinating, messy, horrific – sometimes all at once. Such is the case of the Sephardic Jews of the Iberian Peninsula. The word Sephardic is derived from the Hebrew word for Spain, Sepharad (and variations). In 1492 the Catholic King and Queen of Spain, Ferdinand and Isabel, chose to expel its Jews, who had arrived very early on following the destruction of the Temple in

Jerusalem by the Romans in the first century CE. They could remain if they converted and would be called conversos or New Christians. Portugal would be pressured to follow suit.

I am researching the arrival of these Jews in present day northeastern Mexico who were founders and settlers, but hiding their heritage, in the 16th century of Monterrey and other settlements – right next door to us in South Texas.

One particularly fascinating story is what befell Luis de Carvajal y de la Cueva, a converso, and his sister's family, Crypto-Jews, that is secret Jews, is indeed tragic. His story began with him as a rising star at court in Spain and would end with his death in prison, and with his sister's family executed in Mexico City for relapsing to Judaism, or what the Spanish called, observing the Law of Moses.

Carvajal was born in Mogadouro, Portugal near the Spanish border around 1537 and was educated and partly reared in the home of an aristocrat in Spain. So thorough his education must have been that he learned to speak the Castilian of the upper classes such that he could function at court in Spain and later granted access to King Phillip II of Spain.

In 1579 the king appointed him governor of the newly established province of el Nuevo Reino de Leon, today, Nuevo Leon, with Monterrey as its modern capital.

This province included large areas of Texas and New Mexico as well as the modern Mexican states of Nuevo Leon, Tamaulipas and Coahuila. And because his post included Texas I submit that he should be considered the first governor of Texas.

It should be noted that Carvajal as a New Christian, would, under official policy, be forbidden to enter the new colonies in the Americas and would much less be given a high position. The concern of the crown and the church was that new converts could not be trusted not to return to their Jewish faith, settling in the hinterland, as they came to do. Only Old Christians were officially sanctioned.

But there was a pressing need to settle the northern reaches of New Spain, Christianize the natives and seize treasure. Carvajal convinced the king that he was the man to do it.

At the same time of the appointment the king authorized Carvajal to raise cattle. As many settlers would have some cattle for their personal needs this would seem to have been for the purposes of establishing a large operation, thus requiring the king's signature and seal. Many cattle would over the centuries become free-roaming and be gathered by later settlers. Thus, the genesis of the cattle industry.

Also unusual was that in authorizing Carvajal to recruit 100 families to colonize the new province that no questions would be asked of them, such as their status as Christians, by Spanish officials. This can only mean that many who arrived in the Carvajal flotilla at Tampico, 300 miles south of present-day Brownsville, were either New Christians or still of the Jewish faith, officially barred.

Included among the colonists was his sister's family.

By all accounts Carvajal carried out his assignment thoroughly. But as with many leaders he engendered envy and resentment even among officials. Some may even have suspected that he was a New Christian, again, forbidden in the Americas. But they could not pin anything on him. That he practiced the Catholic faith, at least outwardly, was unquestioned.

But that did not hold true for his sister's family as the case unfolded. Francisca de Carvajal and her children Luis the younger, named for his uncle, Isabel, Leonor and Catalina were arrested in Mexico City on the charge of being Crypto-Jews, secretly practicing Judaism. They underwent years of trial, release following contrition, re-arrest as a result of new accusations, and were eventually executed in 1596. Years later, two other daughters, Mariana and Ana would be executed on the same charges.

Carvajal's crime was that he did not report his sister to the Inquisition. He died in prison in 1591.

His heir, Luis the younger, has received attention recently. He kept a journal with religious thoughts and prayers. That provided the evidence needed to convict him. Decades ago, the journal disappeared from the Archivo General de la Nación in Mexico City. In 2017 it showed up at auction in New York. A collector of Judaica purchased it. Once realizing from experts what it was, he had it digitized by Princeton University where it can be downloaded free, and then had it repatriated to the Mexican archive.

This is one area of my research which will hopefully result in a book. I am studying other families and tracing Sephardic Jews from Spain and Portugal to New Spain, as well as their ancient story in Iberia. Suffice to say now that many South Texas families can trace their lineage to these Sephardic Jews, victims in Iberia and New Spain of religious intolerance of the worst kind.

I can trace my interest in this history to one individual who I met in graduate school at Columbia University in New York – Jackie Kamerow, now Ben-Efraim, a linguist and librarian at the American Jewish University in Los Angeles. She introduced me to Sephardic history of which I knew nothing about. As it turns out she was correct in that I, and I must say, many others, share this lineage.

READ A MORE DETAILED DESCRIPTION OF THIS WORK AT MAYSUBLISHING.COM.

Javier Villarreal

Javier Villarreal holds a BA and MA in Spanish and a Ph.D. in Hispanic Linguistics. His works have been widely published. He retired from Texas A&M University-Corpus Christi in 2015. He writes, practices photography and promotes cultural events in South Texas.

Mis abuelos y yo
(Polaroid Memories)

Don't leave for tomorrow what you can do today,
repeated don Tiburcio, hand-rolling a cigarette
then taking a swig of aguardiente.

I see myself in the mirror of your eyes,
whispered doña Angelita,
cradling my early years with her light.

These words flow like fresh water
like the sweet flavor of cornfield dew
as a never-ending blessing in disguise.

Sometimes I perceive them in the mornings
peeking through the window as a glint of light
and as a whisper of countryside scent at night.

From behind a weathered window,
a young boy peels the dull rind of time
and moved by light finds my eyes.

Pulling into focus from the shadows
like an early sun's gaze on open land,
our smiles leisurely drift across the plains.

This warm moment passes like a summer rain.
Quivering puddles spring to life upon my touch.
Mis abuelos' wisdom airborne in my mind.
A childhood flash before my cloudy winter eyes.

Los abuelos y yo
(Recuerdos en Polaroid)

—*No dejes pa' mañana lo que puedas hacer hoy*,
repetía don Tiburcio, enrollando su tabaco
y apurando un traguito de aguardiente.

—*Eres el espejo donde se ven mis ojos,*
murmuraba doña Angelita,
iluminando mis ojos con los suyos.

Sus consejos brotan como agua prodigiosa.
Como el dulce rocío de milpa por la mañana,
eterna bendición más allá de unas palabras.

A veces, los presiento junto a la puerta.
Otras, los percibo asomando a la ventana,
un suave aroma a campo su presencia.

A través de la distancia asoma un niño.
Tras la ventana retira el polvo de sus ojos.
Luego, se detiene ante los míos que lo observan.

Una sonrisa instintiva se vislumbra,
se asienta como diáfana luz en las pupilas
una pausa ilusoria en el semblante.

El instante efusivo pasa como lluvia veraniega.
Se humedece el pensamiento y un suspiro
fluye de nuevo al manantial de los recuerdos,
agua en remansos donde habitan los abuelos

Jason Bond

Jason Bond is a Corpus Christi native and teaches fourth grade. He lives with his beautiful wife, Rose. When not taking care of his cat and dog, Jason loves to read and write. His hope and dream is that someone else enjoys his imagination.

Just Desserts

"I guess that's it," remarked Officer Gallagher. He stared at the body slumped over the kitchen table. Silence enveloped the room. The small red iridescent clock on the microwave read 8:31 A.M.

Officer Ortiz walked to the table carefully and approached the scene. He grabbed the shoulder of the corpse with his rubber glove covered hand. He pulled the slumped bloated figure back slowly. The body went from being hunched over itself in some obscene prayer to now leaning slouched against the wooden back of the chair. "Oh, yeah! Look at that smile." he replied disgustedly, annoyed.

The widened smile on the pale white body was an image of pure happiness. The skin was translucent. There underneath the ashen skin was a roadmap of blueish veins across the poor man's face. If it were not for the fact that the body was dead, Ortiz would have sworn that the corpse had just won the lottery or something.

"No, not that," Gallagher pointed to the decorative glass on the table. "That."

One the kitchen table was what looked like an ornamental glass from what could have held a milkshake straight from a 1950's soda fountain. Layered inside was white fluffy cream and rich milk chocolate. Smiling between those were layers of fresh ripe raspberries and purple plump blueberries. Officer Gallagher noticed that between the layers of the dessert he could identify, were layers that he could not. There was a thin layer of what first appeared to be caramel, and just below the surface was a layer of something silver and florescent. The colors of the parfait were too bright to be something that was made in this tiny kitchen. The colors seemed to shift and change before Officer Gallagher's eyes.

"Oh yeah, I guess you are right. Stay away from it until we can get someone in here to bag it up." Said Ortiz.

Officer Gallagher had heard all about this new dessert that was making its way around the dark web. The recipe was said to have been taken down dozens of times all around the world, but somehow it kept coming back. And yet, now here it was only a few feet away from him. Calling him.

"That body freaking stinks. I'm going to wait outside in the fresh air until the truck gets here." Officer Ortiz said as he covered his face and walked out of the room.

Soon, Officer Gallagher was alone with the bloated grinning ex-resident of the house. He walked the two steps to take in a closer inspection at the layers of the heavenly dessert. It was rumored to be the most wonderfully created sweet coming from God himself. To taste the parfait was to glimpse heaven. The only side effect was the fact that it was indeed just a glimpse, because one bite brought death. The flavors were also said to be too much for any one person, and the dead body slouching in the kitchen chair beside him was proof.

Officer Gallagher picked up the spoon that was resting on the crumpled napkin. He rhythmically tapped the side of the antique glassware.

The dessert called to him. What was it like to taste heaven? The slowly rotting corpse could no longer share that secret. The bliss that it had once experienced had been taken with him to the grave. Officer Gallagher dipped the spoon into the corner of the glass letting it slide gently down layer after delicious layer.

He picked up the glass and held the dessert up to the sunlight to admire the multi-layered sweetness. The morning light shone through the kitchen window making the glass sparkle like a thousand diamonds.

Officer Gallagher was alone in the silence. He held the spoon up to his lips. "Just a taste." He thought to himself. He just so slightly stuck out his tongue and licked the white fluffiness. The moment the flavors kissed his lips, Officer Gallagher knew that it had all been true. He gulped the dessert, sticking the spoonful deep in his mouth. Gallagher closed his eyes and let the flavors spread not just in his mouth, but through his soul.

The smell and the death of the kitchen faded away around him.

"The colors, all of the wonderful colors." Officer Gallagher said as he raised his hands to heaven and began to slowly spin like a child in a field of wildflowers. "Thank you, Father." Was the last thing he whispered before his dead body fell to the floor with a dull thud.

Jen Deselms

Jen Deselms says she has been surfing badly since moving to the area in 1994 from landlocked states. She posts on Facebook

Old Lady Surf Report

Aug 26, 2020. Unexpected day off. Managed to paddle out to end of pier, a feat in itself for an old lady. Got pummelled, crushed, shot from a cannon and thrashed. Good news was that no old ladies were harmed in the making of this report. And then, Omg. A dolphin. Huge. The first time it leaped, I almost missed it, but then it leaped two more times, body completely out of the water and really close. Only regret was that I was surfing south side alone so there was no one to marvel in the moment with me.

Oct 28, 2020. Woke to 47-degree temps, wind, fog and mist. I couldn't imagine that I would get the motivation to surf. But a hurricane swell in the gulf does strange things. Temp got up to 66. Broke out the wetsuit and luckily could still get in it. Waves were awesome and I beat the working crowd.

Nov 7, 2020. Caught more, bigger, better. Pop-up still sucked but had a couple rides all the way to shore and enough gas in my tank to paddle out four times. And I learned once again how small my town is. A man I don't know said he had seen me in the water several times and then told me exactly where I live. He lives about a block away.

Nov 19, 2020. The Texas Coast means 80 degree air temps in mid-November and the truck next to you may have a cowboy hat on the dash and a surfboard hanging out of the bed.

Nov. 22, 2020. I wasn't really feeling it when I got up before dawn to stroll with the dog. Waves didn't look great and air was cool, but then I saw Magnificent White Beard stretching on the sand. Took the dog home. By the time I returned, he was packing up and I paddled out alone. As I sat on my board, a dolphin's fin appeared. Seconds later another jumped as it surfed a wave. Thanks for the gift, White Beard. May your chin mane continue to wave in the morning breeze.

Dec. 13, 2020. The surf was rolling with a huge crowd hooting and howling as they surfed on the south side of the pier. But the north side was nearly as fine with only three surfers. First wave was a nice drop in, and it formed and reformed all the way in. I had one more glorious ride later during which I felt like my board was dancing up and down the face forever. Did it look as good as it felt? Probably not. Left shortly after the sky turned a deep blue gray, the water an eerie green and the wind howled more than the surfers.

Dec 23, 2020. Totally needed some attitude adjustment and the company of my usual surf buddy. On my first ride I nabbed a fisherman's line at my waist but managed to grab it and fling it over my head and keep on cruising. Felt like a rock star. On a paddle out toward the end of the session some tourists cheered us on. Felt like a rock star again. But as usual I also took a bunch of water up the nose. It got a bit chilly.

March 16, 2021. Surf was slow and mushy but rideable. For the first time in several years, I hit myself in the face with my board. Missed my eye by a fraction of an inch, but my cheekbone is a bit tender. Got tangled up with a fisherman who seemed at least pleasant about nearly reeling in the giant jenfish.

May 13, 2021. Water was a clear dark green with little mounds just big enough for some fun rides. Was joined by several fellow gray hairs. Glad they joined me because I spotted a fin in the water twice and couldn't be sure what it was. Had I been alone I might have paddled in, but in a group I stayed until my fingers turned to prunes. All was right with the world.

May 31, 2021. I had some epic wipeouts. Caught a couple, but horrible pop-ups led to rides on knees. And it was cold. Really cold. My blubber didn't do much. Nearly broke the water heater upon my return.

July 11, 2021. Shouldn't have gone to the fish fry before paddling out. Also was thwarted by messy waves and a nagging thumb injury. Still grabbed several ugly rides with slow pop-ups. No style points awarded today. Stopped before I made my thumb worse.

Aug. 20, 2021. Lots of shortboarders crushing it, and one old lady occasionally getting crushed. Paddled out to the end of the pier four times before catching the elusive wave of the day all the way to shore. Did I look good? Only to the newbie gal who asked me for some paddling out tips, but the ride felt good. No, it felt great.

Read more "Old Lady Surf Report" at MaysPublishing.com

Jo Ann Sanderson

JoAnn Sanderson was born in Iowa, received a Master's degree in English Education at Southern Illinois University, and taught in Illinois public schools for many years. After she retired, she researched possible places to re-locate and chose Corpus Christi, Texas.

The Incident at Swan Pond

If you had been sitting on a bench at Patriot's Park in Lewisville, Illinois, at 4:30 p.m., on June 9th, you would have seen Mayor Sam Samuels stretching before he began his two mile run on the nature trail that wound through the park. Since he was facing east, you would have known by the directional arrows posted along the trails that he was headed down the path that ran by Swan Pond.

But if you had, instead, wandered down to the shopping area, you might have seen Angie looking at the apparel in the town's only women's boutique, The Trendy Threads. You would be able to watch her change numerous times into two outfits--a purple dress with a peplum bodice and a black sequined jumpsuit. But you might not have known she was deciding what to wear for her dinner date in the evening at the Lewisville Inn.

If you had then taken a short drive to the Old Town Square to visit the meticulously restored courthouse which housed the police headquarters, you would have seen Officer Perez, who had been on the force for ten years and Officer Cornelius, who had been hired only six months ago, typing information onto routine forms. If you had wandered into the office, you would have heard Perez and Cornelius talking about their boss, Humphrey McDuff, Chief of Police.

"He's been acting pretty weird lately," Perez spoke as he typed. "Yesterday he spent half the day gazing out the window, muttering to himself."

Cornelius stopped typing. "I don't know how long this can go on. We can't keep covering for him like we have been. I've been hearing some rumors about him around town."

"Rumors, innuendos, gossip, conjectures, hearsay, scuttlebutt. This town thrives on this stuff, Corny. We spend a lot of time and effort separating fact from fiction."

Suddenly, Chief McDuff entered their office. "I want you guys in my office, *muy pronto*."

If you had followed them into the chief's office, you would have witnessed the chief's strange behavior that Officers Perez and Cornelius had been discussing.

You would have seen Chief McDuff sit down behind his desk, the officers settle into chairs facing him, and heard the chief announce, "You will soon be called by a 9-1-1 dispatcher to investigate a possible crime scene."

You might have observed how the confused officers shifted in their seats and heard Officer Perez ask, "Excuse me, sir, you said the call had not yet been made?"

"You heard me correctly, Perez. You will respond to the call by going to Patriot's Park, where the body of Mayor Sam Samuels will have been discovered by a jogger running on the trail which leads to Swan Pond. The body will be found lying under some trees a few feet from the 10th marker. You will determine that the mayor had been shot at point blank range with a 9MM Glock, one bullet straight through the heart and one bullet to the head."

Perez persisted, "But, sir, how would you know . . . ? "

"I suppose you want to know what the victim was wearing, too," McDuff interrupted.

Hoping to take the heat off Officer Perez, Officer Cornelius intervened. "No, sir. We just don't understand how you know we're going to get this call."

You might have sensed that the officers were not accustomed to questioning the source or the validity of the information the chief reported. But the officers had indicated that until recently, they had not seen the chief muttering alone at his desk, tossing police reports in the waste basket, and staring for hours at the county map hanging on the wall by his filing cabinet.

Showing no sign of being offended, Chief McDuff began describing the victim's clothing.

"He was wearing navy blue jogging pants and a navy blue short sleeved T-shirt with a white stripe running down the right side. And although you are not detectives, I'll tell you that the murderer's motive for killing Mayor Samuels was that he had been cavorting around town with the murderer's wife. Since there were several joggers beginning their five o'clock run, I expect the call will be coming in soon." Chief McDuff stood and paced around the room. He walked to the window and opened and shut the blinds several times before slipping an unlighted cigar between his lips.

Perez looked up at the ceiling, and Cornelius looked down at the floor, considering the details the chief had reported. After a brief silence, Officer Perez suggested, "Well, Corny, we'd better head out there and check this situation out."

The chief laughed. "Hold on a minute, boys. He's already dead.

No need to rush."

If you had been observing the officers closely, you would have also sensed that they had agreed that they had matters to take care of before they went to the park.

Then you would have seen Perez and Cornelius stand and walk slowly toward him as Perez announced, "Chief, you're under arrest for the murder of Mayor Sam Samuels. It is necessary for us to handcuff you to the desk while we arrange for support to handle this situation."

"Well, Perez, I guess you'd better read me my rights. And since you insist on adhering to the proper protocols, will you hand me my phone to call my lawyer? Oh, and will one of you fellas call my wife? Tell Angie to forget about meeting the mayor at the Lewisville Inn tonight. Tell her he had to deal with some unforeseen emergency. She hates to be kept waiting, you know."

If you had chosen to leave the office after the two men handcuffed McDuff to the desk and had followed Perez and Cornelius into the hallway, you would have heard the anxiety in Cornelius's voice.

"Perez, the chief is crazy as hell. I don't know what to believe about what we'll find out there at Swan Pond."

After hearing this conversation, you would have probably rushed over to Swan Pond to see if the mayor were dead or merely suffering from a gun shot wound. But, perhaps, you would have found him sitting on a bench, drinking from his bottle of electrolyte-infused water, having completed his two mile run, fit as a fiddle.

Jimmy Willden

Jimmy Willden is an award-winning filmmaker, journalist, musician, writer, and Corpus Christi native. Currently, he's the editor of two newspapers, co-owner of a production company, and founder of Corpus Christi Songwriters.

Excerpt from **"Bright Static"**

The television screen swims in black and blue static once more. Small faces are barely recognizable amidst the interrupted signal that sends the black and white pictures back into its twisted dance before me.

Once again wearing our marital comforter like a shaw, I sit on the floor before *his* beastly burgundy television studying all of the dots dancing on the screen over smiling faces and sad faces and angry faces and hollow faces. I swear – these faces are all starting to merge into one, bright and electric face – but I can't be sure just yet. For now, however, they are all singing along to that altogether beautiful pulsating rhythm, vibrating in and through me, just like the water droplets sending ripples through an ocean of bath water, just like all of those reflections refracting all the light that remains. I see it all. I feel it all.

Until I don't.

"Momma…"

I blink and look up beyond the blue static to find my beloved boy wrapped in his very own blanket shaw, once again, shivering.

"Momma…I'm cold."

In the backyard, with the sun once again just below the horizon as if it's too afraid to announce the arrival of the brand new day, I stand beside the house, and find the ax right where I last saw it. It hasn't been moved or touched, nor has the firewood.

"*I'll bring some in, in a minute*," were the last words my beloved husband had said on the matter, twenty-four hours ago.

This burning from within hasn't slept at all, it was just quietly building in its intensity and now begging to be heard and to be felt in its entirety. I grab the ax, with my sweet boy standing behind me. I feel him watching me, as that burning rage from within finally finds its way to the surface and guides the ax high up into the air above me, with my grip tightening around its handle. I scream so loud my ears ring, and then the rage sends the ax violently down, slamming into a piece of firewood placed on the ground before me. The force of the chopping reverberates through the handle and right into my hands. I feel alive. I feel new – as the wood splits in two.

Joel Ortiz

Joel Jay Ortiz has been reading, writing, and performing poetry since 1991. He started at various open mikes, reading poetry with musicians, and then continued when open mike with spoken word began appearing. The following are excerpts from **Corpitos: A Sadness**

Welcome to Corpitos.

From bayfest being canceled during lame hurricanes,
That never landed, to
Cops shooting more brown skin men since I can remember

They call this the toughest land in the west, it was a hard place, with a
Hot sun following your every move, scaring your shadow into the gulf.

I thought it was normal,

Doesn't everybody get questioned 'do you speak english?'
Or, "when was the last time you were in prison?'

That's Corpus for some, for others, it's a paradise with ghetto trees
Populating the scenery, sun-beaten skin looking like leather, on some,
And don't get me started on the mosquitos!

But one thing I can tell you friend,
You will not leave Corpus Christi hungry,
Nor blessed.

El Catrin

Always a cigarette, in his hand or his mouth, but notwithstanding,
There is always a cigarette.

For a while it was bidi's, indian rolled tobacco, looking like a mini cornucopia
Satisfying the smokers urge to go with the smokers cough,

Dressed to the nines, in baggy chinos, plain white t shirt, and
Stacey Adams

Plus the fedora.

That's him walking the beats, on everyone's breath as he
Walks by, eyes downward cast,

El Gallo

There he struts, like some brown Travolta, tres viejos in his hair,
Demanding a tortilla in the chinese buffet,
Once he brought his own music, Bach on the tape recorder, on full blast
For all the other patrons to admire along.
Sometimes, he sports a mullet, sometimes it looks like a haircut that is half
Finished.
Always a connoisseur of things, but doesnt know how to let others in his
circle,
He will get the girl, by the dawn's early night, he will get the girl,
Or he will fight you because there is nothing else to do.
He will claw your eyes out, watch out, he fights dirty,
But he will get you an Uber to get you home safely, for he is
A gentleman of a different stance, as he stands in your house
And with mere looks, he impregnates everybody with a desire
To live.

Este Vato knows how to live. He drinks the finest cervezas this
Side of the river, he has honeys by the wayside,
He gets deals like you don't know. He will bust out the snow,
But only on occasions when the *juras* are not around.
How he knows the *juras* not around, he tells us his
Grandfather is a curandero, and we all stand in awe
Of such folk-like stories, we believe them late into
Middle age, waking us up in the night, still sitting on your chest.
Stealing your breath.

El gallo is a good friend to have, he backs you up, even when the
World shits on you, he will come and brighten your day, he will come and
Make you laugh. He will come in his new Mustang, and he will crash it
Outside the dope house.
That's the gallo, and no matter what, he gets up for work the next morning
As if he went to sleep at nine.

Apocalyptic by Philip Perez. Model Candi Green

John Kemmerly

John Kemmerly grew up in South Louisiana, worked in restaurants, sold real estate, and owned a secondhand bookstore in Galveston, Texas. He has published in Psychology Today magazine, Modern Dog magazine, and others. Currently, he lives near Rockport, Texas.

Hemingway in Port Aransas

Various accounts of Ernest Hemingway's visit to Port Aransas still linger on the Island. Some are credible, some not. We know that he showed up here July 20th, 1957, with his friend Arnold Samuelson. Arnold was a young aspiring writer who had hitchhiked and ridden boxcars to Hemingway's home in Key West, Florida, to, as he later wrote, "Learn from the best damn writer there ever was." The two men hit it off, and after a few months of fishing in Key West, they took the boat to Port A.

They made the 850 nautical mile trip on Hemingway's boat, the Pilar. The Pilar was a 38-foot sports fisherman that Hemingway modified by lowering the transom twelve inches and adding a wooden roller to help with landing large fish. They docked at Fisherman's Wharf on a Saturday afternoon without notifying the press or anyone else; however the word of his arrival quickly spread throughout the Island. Locals gathered around the famous author to ask questions, shake his hand, and take pictures. Hemingway, they said, was patient enough but soon started looking for a fight. Not a real fight but rather a boxing match, an event, he announced, to stir up a little excitement. Several opponents were discussed along with size and speed, and most importantly, who would be brave enough to actually fight the great man.

Locals soon agreed on Big Nate, a black deckhand who worked on the Scat Cat and was rumored to be the toughest man on the Island. Nate had grown up in Galveston, Texas, the hometown of the first black heavyweight champion of the world, Jack Johnson. He had been friends with Mr. Johnson and watched him fight in battle royals, which were illegal and dangerous but lucrative for both the promoter and the winner. At the Galveston City Docks, behind rows of warehouses, they would sink four posts in the ground and loop ropes around it. Then, anywhere from four to eight black men would step into the ring blindfolded and punch it out until only one was left standing.

Nate had never fought in a battle royal but had done his share of fighting around the wharves of Port Aransas. Not only was he brave, but he also had a sense of humor and often repeated a story about the world champion. He and Jack Johnson, along with two of Johnson's girlfriends, were driving to Florida on vacation. The two women sat up front with Jack in his Cadillac convertible. It was spring and the top was down. Jack wore a maroon mink coat and sped through Alabama at ninety miles an hour. A deputy pulled him over for speeding, and Nate, according to the story he told, heard the deputy talking about a fifty dollar fine. This was back when a hamburger cost ten cents, a chocolate malt a nickel. Johnson didn't seem upset by the deputy's outrageous demand. Nate assumed Mr. Johnson had simply misheard the amount.

Johnson opened his glove box to look for some cash, while the deputy waited at the side of the road, a smirk on his face. All Jack could find were stacks of hundreds, the payment from a recent fight. He rifled through his stack, looking for something smaller, and ended up giving the deputy a crisp new hundred dollar bill. At first he was too shocked to respond. He had never seen a hundred dollar bill before and tried to explain that he couldn't possibly make change nor did he know anyone else who could. Jack listened patiently and buttoned up his mink coat before telling the officer, "Keep it all. I'll be coming back the same way."

Beer at Shorty's

Hemingway and his friend Arnold hung around the dock, meeting locals. The Scat Cat was still out in the Gulf and wouldn't return until late afternoon, so Hemingway asked about a bar, said he'd satisfy his thirst before taking on Big Nate. A throng of fishermen led him to Shorty's, where they gathered together on the porch and introduced Ernest to Miss Rose, the owner. Miss Rose was an attractive, well-respected woman, who had declined the attentions of most of the men in Port Aransas. People wondered if things would be different for the great writer, if he'd have better luck.

The bartender served beer as fast as he could open them, while Miss Rose stayed busy icing down more bottles. Mr. Hemingway wanted to know about the local fishing, specifically marlin and sailfish. The men discussed baits and blue water along with various fishing techniques and state records.

"Do fish hear?" one of the locals asked.

This started a big debate with everyone weighing in on the argument. Miss Rose watched as the debate grew louder. Many of the fishermen still wore fillet knives on their belt, something Miss Rose didn't allow inside her bar. At this point though, she was more concerned with serving her customers.

"Fish cannot hear a lick. They only feel vibrations," someone said.

"Of course they can hear," a local boat captain announced. "You rev your engines or bang the surface with a paddle and the Ling come to the surface."

"See, that's what I'm talking about," the man argued, "vibrations not sound."

Hemingway ordered another beer and settled the argument. "Both men are correct," he announced. "Fish can hear sounds surprisingly well, which are nothing more than vibrations moving through the water. Yet most fish are not attracted to noise. Here's what I mean, and I learned this from paying attention to my own mistakes. How many of you have ever raised a billfish, had the great fish take a look around and then back off?"

"It happened this morning," a man leaning against the railing said.

"Ralph, your baits ain't purdy enough," someone called out, spawning laughter.

"Were your baits fresh and riding right?" Hemingway asked.

"Sure they were."

"And yet the billfish somehow figured out the game?"

The man nodded his head in agreement.

"I'll tell you what happened," Hemingway explained. "Your crew probably yelled 'fish up,' or maybe someone rushed across the deck stomping too hard. Both will scare off a smart fish."

At some point Ernest grew bored with the conversation and began looking for someone to match his skills at a game of billiards. He called over a man wearing white shrimp boots. "Young man," he said, "how's your pool game?"

The shrimper responded confidently, "Sir, I was conceived on that pool table."

Ernest hesitated and took a closer look at him. "Son?" he asked.

The guy paused … "Dad?"

Ernest sprung from his bar stool and hugged the young man. It was a happy occasion for everyone until Miss Rose, who was cracking block ice with a wooden mallet, looked up and said, "No, I think not."

Mr. Hemingway laughed it off while keeping an affectionate eye on Miss Rose, whispering an occasional devotion in her ear.

Advice to Writers

Big Nate was fishing offshore totally unaware that Ernest Hemingway would be waiting for him at the dock.

"Sir," one of the fishermen asked Ernest, "I write every day, but who should I read to improve my writing, other than you of course?"

"Read everyone," Hemingway told him, "so you know who you have to beat. But don't try to beat Shakespeare. He's unbeatable."

On the trip over from Key West, sitting beside the master, Arnold had received plenty of good writing advice. He was careful to remember everything Hemingway told him: "Write what you know, and don't write anything before you know it. Only write the tip of the iceberg and leave the rest underwater ... For me, I write one page of masterpiece to ninety-one pages of junk, then I throw away the junk."

Flat's Lounge

Ernest wanted a Papa Doble like the ones he'd had at the Floridita in Havana. Someone suggested they all go next door to The Flats Lounge. Inside the bar, Hemingway surveyed the large dark room and decided to lead his entourage to the rear corner. He introduced himself to the bartender Howie and asked about the drink from Cuba. "A Papa Doble. Do you know it?"

Back then, Howie was, without argument, the best bartender on the Island. While making Hemingway's signature drink, he quoted the recipe. "Two shots of Bacardi rum. Half a lime. Splash of grapefruit juice and six drops of marasca cherry liqueur. Blend it with shaved ice and serve it with a head of seafoam."

Ernest was pleased. He respected any man who took his job seriously and excelled in his craft. "Weren't you a bartender on South Padre Island?" Hemingway asked.

"Yes sir," Howie answered.

"I think you knew my granddaughter, Mariel."

"It was a good time and I met a lot of people back then," Howie said.

Hemingway tilted back his Papa Doble. "I'm not upset with you, young man, just asking."

"Yes sir, I knew her well."

The Big Fight

Big Nate would return to the dock soon, so after another round of drinks, Hemingway and his entourage went to go find him. At the dock, men carried boxes of fresh caught fish from the boat to the oyster shell parking lot where a large sign read, "Port Aransas, Fishing Capitol of Texas." Deckhands hung fish from the sign. Tourists from the Scat Cat stood next to their catch, while someone from the newspaper took pictures.

Hemingway, along with his new friends, entered the parking lot to find Nate. And there he was, a large muscled black man in a white T-shirt splattered with fish blood. Nate grabbed a king mackerel with one hand and spiked it on a nail. "Let the man finish his work," Hemingway said, but it was too late. People rushed over with the proposition. Nate looked over at Ernest, giving him a hard study before saying, "I ain't gonna beat up no old white man."

Nevertheless, Ernest and Nate were soon introduced. "It will just be an exhibition match, some entertainment for the locals," Ernest told him.

Once the fight was agreed to, a kid on a bike went racing through Old Town yelling the news to people sitting on their porches. They came from all directions to gather around the bait stand at Fisherman's Wharf. Some were drinking beer, others were placing bets. When no one could find two pairs of boxing gloves, just one oversized glove with dry rot leather, someone suggested rags. "We could wrap their fists up with some oil rags."

Ernest and Nate discussed it and decided yes, rags would be okay. While their hands were being carefully wrapped, someone found a brass bell behind the net maker's garage. After a discussion, the Postmaster was nominated as the official the timekeeper. A shirtless man in overalls used a hoe to scrape a square boundary in the oyster shells. "You all can do your fighting here."

Ernest wore short pants and deck shoes. Nate wore what he had on, jeans and a bloody t-shirt.

The bell sounded and the two men circled each other. Nate threw a jab that didn't reach its target. Ernest tossed a bomb, a big right hand as if he intended to end the fight right there, but Nate was quick and ducked out of the way. Various onlookers called out instructions to the fighters. "Nate, counter with a left hook!" ... "Come on Hem, throw another big right!"

Nate landed the first solid punch, a quick jab to the forehead, but while Nate was in close, Hemingway stepped in even closer and dug a left fist into Nate's ribs. Shock and pain folded his face into a grimace, but he quickly brushed off the blow and stayed in there, throwing body shots of his own. When round one ended, both men were breathing hard, dripping sweat. Ernest called out for a beer and searched the crowd for Miss Rose.

In the next round, Nate danced from one side to the other, trying to circle his opponent and tire him out. Ernest pivoted left and then right, always staying directly in front of Big Nate. As the seconds ticked off, punches were landed by both men, but Ernest's punches seemed to do the most damage, sending a trickle of blood dripping from Nate's chin. When the round ended, Ernest announced he would go one more. Arnold used a towel to wipe sweat from his face. Someone gave him a swig from a bottle of brandy.

The bell rang for round three. Nate started landing his quick jab, frustrating Ernest, who wasn't always fast enough to block it or get out of the way. He was getting tired, too, clinging on to Nate for an occasional rest. Near the end of the round, Ernest found the strength to rock his opponent with a left hook to the chin. Nate staggered backward. It looked like Ernest was about to move in and finish him off, but the bell sounded and the fight was over.

The crowd cheered for the fighters. Ernest lifted Nate's hand declaring the fight a draw. People clapped and whistled, while the two men hugged and congratulated each other. Earnest unwrapped the rags from his fists and slipped some money into Nate's pocket, thanking him for a brave and fair fight.

Everything in Texas

Miss Rose and her bartenders were ready for the rush, having spent the past hour icing beer, refilling bowls with peanuts, jars with pickled eggs.

"We appreciate the business," Miss Rose told Ernest.

"Not a problem," He said, and leaned forward to ask something in private. Miss Rose only smiled without offering a satisfactory answer. Later, Islanders would speculate about this brief exchange. Had she rejected him? Miss Rose went on to live a long and successful life, and even though she was often pressured, she never betrayed the confidence of Earnest Hemingway.

Historians speculated about Miss Rose and what would have happened if she had become his fifth wife. Scholars say that his greatest novels were inspired by new found love, and that Hemingway sought out a new woman each time his writing powers waned. Miss Rose, at the time, had her hands full running three bars and apparently was not charmed by the author's attention. So when Hemingway failed to produce a final novel before he died, some scholars held Miss Rose responsible, claiming "That woman had no sense of history."

Arnold Samuelson wouldn't write much either after this. In spite of having the best mentor money could buy, he never found his voice as a writer. It was sad when, late in life, melancholia overwhelmed him. He isolated himself from friends and family and pretty much lost his mind, sitting naked in his front yard unwilling to communicate. His daughter said he had become stuck in the past, trapped with his memories of Ernest Hemingway.

They had stayed in Port Aransas for a week, Ernest and Arnold, fishing every morning, drinking every afternoon, but they never went back to Shorty's. On the return trip to Key West, they were standing on the flybridge looking out over the Gulf of Mexico when Arnold asked, "What about Miss Rose? What happened?"

Hemingway paused for a moment before answering, "Everything in Texas either bites, sticks, stings, or breaks your heart."

Sand Pail on the Beach by **John Morris**

John Morris

Most mornings John Morris heads to the beach with his camera. His stunning photography is viewable on his website. Yet, his writing is every bit as extraordinary as his photos. He posts photos and commentary on Facebook **https://www.facebook.com/683Photograph** and Instagram **@jmorris683photography** and his website **https://www.jmorris683photography.com/**
See color versions of John's work on the Kindle version of Corpus Christi Writers 2022

From John Morris's Facebook posts

Castaway - I'm called to the beach seemingly every day...there are exceptions...duty calls...other priorities...stuff happens...but most every morning I can be found on the beach greeting the new day. Some mornings the outcomes seem obvious, splendid colors, light winds, towering clouds, reflections on mirror-like waters...and then there are those mornings where it would seem that there is nothing...but really there is always something...if one only looks...a castaway waiting to be found. Is that not just like our own lives, even on the darkest day, there is color...some small hint that it will be OK if we keep moving...our heart and eyes working in concert...knowing that it is out there...just awaiting our discovery.

Coastal Colors – One of those special mornings that almost didn't happen. Usually from my deck in the wee hours of the morning the subtle hints of coastal color emerge…either giving me encouragement to get out…or like this morning, with very little showing I was thinking it was going to be a bust. As I busied myself on other early morning chores, by chance I glimpsed out, and things had changed…so off to the beach I went. When I first arrived, my attention was drawn to the play of light along the shoreline, and the small waves kissing the shoreline…if I could only get it all to come together…those little elements…that make a shot. As the sun peeked over the distant pier, the shoreline and the beach break waves were painted in gold, and then it happened…high above a few pink cotton candy clouds drifted into the shot…completing coastal colors!
Today was one of exceeded expectations, maybe one of those special nudges…when we listen with our heart…we see things we might have missed…had we only looked with our eyes.

Towering Above – As the morning transitioned from the black of night, to the blue hour of dawn, the horizon began to brighten…offering a glimpse of what might come…if only. It seemed that the pier was going to be the spot as I watched a towering cloud, occasionally lit from within by flashes of lightening; though for the shot I had in mind, the cloud had slid too far inland, so a quick adjustment put me at the south jetty, with the cloud towering high above St. Joe Island, casting bands of gold reflecting across the channel highlighting a sportfisher heading towards the horizon in calm seas and light winds…a promise of a new day.

Silent "Leave only Footprints" - This morning I was drawn south, the farther you go the less evidence of people...you actually don't have to go far...a beach that feels somewhat wild still exists...a beach with sea oats, a naturally contoured beach and dunes, where most of the footprints are those of the nocturnal animals that scurry about the dunes...the hunters and the hunted...leaving only footprints as evidence of their passage. Can we maybe just try a bit harder to avoid leaving our mark wherever we go...tread lightly...be a little more "aware" of our passage and its effect as we cross paths.

The Walk of Life by **Ricardo Ruiz**

Ricardo's work is featured in The Cheech Marin Center

FIRST LINES (MORE OR LESS) REDUX
BY WILLIAM MAYS

WHERE HAVE YOU GONE. Here I am. Call me. Before Covid-19 We drank the moonshine down. THE NEXT MORNING AFTER MASS A poem began as a speck of dust. He was going to have to kill The Chihuahua Desert AND *The tree is hemorrhaging sap.* **When I die** **Sneezing, wheezing, coughing, hacking** Staying in the present drains the life right out of me. **Devon jumped** BECAUSE MY DAUGHTER, EMILY, HAD MOVED TO SAUDI ARABIA. Think the first time I entered The Blue Tequila Cantina **Seagulls funneled over the houses crying.** I RAISED HIS HAGGARD FRAME When Rhonda first opened *The China cups.* **Would you still love me** *if I'm walking northeast along Highway 43* FROM BAYFEST. **Crack, crack, crack** **Whomp!** ECHO TIDE

Jon Gregory

Jon Gregory worked for The Fort Worth Star-Telegram for 18 years. His poems, short stories and essays have been published in numerous magazines and journals.

SOMETIMES THE ONLY SONG A MAN HEARS IS HIS ANGER

At night, dreams flash by like slide shows.
But the frames are alive and move to a ghostly cadence.
Figures of the past dancing in and out of the picture
In cinematic jump cuts.
A dimly lit flicker of nonsequiturs.
A woman I once loved and lost appears and speaks softly,
And the only song I can hear is my own sorrow.
Then, flash -- the scene changes,
Like someone flicked the carousel
To a rural homestead, with Mestizo hired hands in tow,
A clan of people so poor
They only know essentials.
And the sky over the homestead
Turns from a deep cool blue
To a swirling cold gray.
Twin tornadoes dig viciously into the northern horizon.
A woman in the kitchen, a grandmother,
And a man in overalls, a grandfather,
Gather us, hired hands and all,
To crawl into the cellar.
But I can't take my eyes off the storm,
Even as they call and call for me.
The twisters draw closer and closer,
And the only song I can hear is my own madness.
Then, flash -- the scene changes.
And I hear the suburban concerto of an old friend,
A boy too privileged to know anything of essentials,
An innocent heir to a soiled fortune.
And in my trance I've forgotten that he no longer exists.
But the lyrics linger in the dream theater
As we down ancient beers in honor of the lost day.
And the only song I can hear is his naivete.
Then, flash -- the scene changes

To a dingy room and the flicker
Of an old TV set, black and white,
The kind you have at the beginning
And the end of your life.
I'm alone, watching the ghostly parade
And the only song I can hear is my anger.

Joseph Wilson

Joseph Wilson taught Senior English Advanced Placement, Film Studies, and Creative Writing at Richard King High School for 42 years.

Swimming Lessons

Tossing me up up up
Like I was a dart
Or an easter egg or
A little blue bag of sand
I remember

Tightening my toes
Hitting the surface of Lake Cline
And water going up my nose
Into my eyes
Turning my shorts into an upside-down parachute

Spitting out the brown mud water
And screaming out what passed for curses
Dazed and animal-happy
When I was six and constantly
Wondering where my father was

Throwing me off the floating dock
Like I was a football
Or a seed from a silver maple tree or
His little white-blonde angel
I remember

Slicing the humid Indiana air
My slender body arcing down into the sparkling lake
My wet face gleaming in the sun
My arms spreading out to the sky like a penitent
I remember Walt

Swimming the length of the lake
My step-father Walt

Taking huge breaths of air
Long long winged-butterflies
Drafting deep

Laughing on the way up
Laughing on the way up
Laughing on the way up

Amarone with Antipasto and Lana

we first met in a high school hallway as fellow literature teachers
she was experiencing a daring hard dangerous divorce
from a viet nam syndrome police sergeant
who slept with a loaded pistol who threatened her with
"I'm going to blow your bitch head off"
I feared for her
I feared for myself because I don't own a gun
and I feared I would end up just being a safe bridge for her

tall graceful curvaceous italiana from chicago
swimmer with long lashes over deep brown river water eyes
the most physically bella woman I ever loved was lana
on my 33rd birthday she gifted me a striking gold
gucci watch tri-colored with geometric motif
three months later when she broke up with me
I hid the watch away in a distant drawer
under my grandmother's purple silk handkerchief

but we shared six months of trauma-infused fun
close dancing free jazz at club robert
kissing sessions at south bluff park
listening to joni while cuddling on her couch
touching toes under the lunch table
making slow love to bach cello solos and
quick love in the elevator at the san antonio art museum
lana taught me to linger over antipasto

and order another bottle of amarone
that most perfect red rich robust wine from lana's verona
(which I cannot afford today)
to marry with charley swanson's special
spicy family pizza at lucianos restaurant
a month after she broke it off
lana went to a post office station to mail me a postcard
when a street person jumped in front of her

dropped his jeans and said
"I'm going to bitch fuck you"
she zigzagged around him
and when safely home under covers called me crying
I sped to her apartment
hugged her like the brother she didn't have
caressed her like the lover that I no longer was
stayed the night but it was over in two weeks

later in the spring
she met a navy pilot and at semester's end
they married and moved to san diego
for quite a long time thinking about lana
was so painful that I couldn't
answer her letters from california
that I couldn't say her name out loud
without becoming dizzy

I was happy for her happiness
I smile when she comes to mind now
the watch was in a cabinet with dead swatch watches
untouched for decades
until I took it in for repair last week
the jeweler called yesterday
left this message
"your gorgeous watch is repaired and ready for pick-up"

Corpus Christi Bay at Night Belinda Aguilar

Joshua Bridgwater Hamilton

Joshua Bridgwater Hamilton lives in Corpus Christi, TX. He holds a PhD in Spanish poetry from Indiana University and, currently, he is an MFA Poetry candidate at Texas State University. He has two chapbooks: *Rain Minnows* (Gnashing Teeth Publishing) and *Slow Wind* (Finishing Line Press). His poetry appears in such journals as Windward Review, Voices de la Luna, Tiny Seed Journal, Amarillo Bay, The Dillydoun Review and San Antonio Review.

Tools for Shedding Skin

Vernal reunion in a pastel
country exceeds inner sanctums—
tune the ear to homecoming
and feel the slow tile of balance
restore timidity.

Spread shapeless maps of summer
on a hoary oak tabletop: diary
of spent movement, neurotic fear,
airplanes subsuming topographic
traces. Mexico City appears
like a kinetic street mass; no
beginning no end just patches
clearing slightly in the massive
fog of humanity –

Avenida Revolución, El Zócalo,
Coyoacán & El Parque
de Chapultepec – to the south,
Cuernavaca, to the north,
ruins of Teotihuacán. Web
of ghostpaths shaped by bare
feet: lines tracing the age
of palm and lava.

Hot blur of glances, retinal
inquisition thickens the scarce air
in metro cars: a pointillistic
impression of identity painted
in massive surges, faces
carved in brilliant relief,
the few islands of conversation,
a curious smile –
seek them out each day,
hungry and eager
to name a friend.

Try to build stones out of bones,
trace blood into a solid
architecture of longing.
But the affinity for structure
fills hunger with walls and squares
until the straight edge breaks down
into volcanic layers. Stand
in the middle of Delegación Benito
Juárez, a pile of rubble
that clatters between seismic rifts.

No longer fluent in the descendent
flesh of words, the parley pattered
with an infinitive overlap,
dressed in a suit of verbs –
not a gentleman so much as an army
of dandelion seeds choking
the pockets, living rooms,
and river valleys of a mute
scarlet resplendent
in mythology.

Window Veil

Dandelion seeds catch
in a web swayed
by afternoon breeze.

The house spider gauges
silk networks
with toothpick legs:

sinister thrums
relay victims' fits
after tangling filament.

But today the lines jitter
with weather and not
spasms away from death.

Later, the seeds' flutter
will loosen, crown gothic
abandon and suspend

ragged decay out-
side the second
floor window pane

where the domestic
arachnid risked air
and fertile bodies far

from dirt
or grass.

Reality by William Mays

John Meza

John Meza writes poems and builds bridges. He also takes stunning pictures. Poem and photo by John Meza

Brown Eyed girl

Brown eyed girl
With a rose tattoo
Plump like peaches
Late summer orchard hips
Carving suns
Through moonlight

Do you always write poetry
In a bar?

No, sometimes I write
In the dark, as I sleep
Other times I write
On the beach at sunrise
Mostly
I write about brown eyed
Girls with rose tattoos
And plump hips like
Late summer peaches

Can I buy you a drink?

Whiskey, neat

True story
By One Deep

I prefer the scent
fingers stroked
a tangled kiss
You and I
we lost
Sur del la frontera
dark roots
brown eyed girl
with a rose tattoo
plump like peaches
summer orchard

Juan Perez

Juan Manuel Pérez, a Mexican-American poet of indigenous descent and a Poet Laureate for Corpus Christi, Texas (2019-2020), is the author of several books of poetry including, PLANET OF THE ZOMBIE ZONNETS Seasons 1 & 2 (Hunger Buzzard Press, 2021). The award-winning poet, history teacher, and Pushcart Nominee, is also a member of the Horror Writers Association, the Science Fiction Poetry Association, and the Military Writers Society of America. Juan worships his Creator and chases chupacabras in the South Texas Coastal Bend Area.

21.

Thirty years ago, a funny story
I'm not saying that it happened to me
I'm not saying that it happened at all
someone smoked a camel in the desert
lit it up despite the ordered blackout
what's so amusing about that you ask?
two night-watchmen hear some nearing footsteps
then demand the assigned, nightly password
nothing responds as the sounds come closer
three-spurt rounds, then something falls to the ground
apparently, camels speak no English
do they taste like chicken? maybe they do
true or not, yet in anyone's version
the camel never makes it out alive

23.

Thirty years ago, thinking of you, Bob
thinking of those that went through this with me
you stood out most in all the things we did
fellow Texan, fellow sci-fi lover
fellow tent mate and an avid reader
now I ain't proposing, falling in love
but telling sick jokes helped us pass the time
when I was angry, you stood to quell me
in arguments, you were the steady hand
like that mailman conspiracy I had
I hope that brother forgives me one day
I was just missing my wife's love letters
I can only laugh, how stupid it was
yet, we stood together, last ones back home

25.

Thirty years ago, Meals Ready to Eat
lots of us knocked them down during the war
and yes, nothing beats a good, old, hot meal
but sealed meals you could carry were a steal
I grew fond of them as the days went by
dedicating this space to list favorites:
pork with rice dipped in sweet barbecue sauce
corned beef hash with red, hot, Tabasco sauce
potatoes au Gratin warmed by the sun
chicken ala king and fit for one too
crackers with cheese spread, a course by itself
beef stew and ham slice, also on record
stuck in any conflict, they hit the spot
for hungry Men always Ready to Eat

40.

Thirty years ago, a deck of fresh cards
red queen of hearts to a black king of clubs
enduring sound of a sturdy shuffle
blackjack of spades to a red queen of hearts
indulging lonely probabilities
red ten of diamonds to blackjack of spades
something needed while enduring the war
black nine of clubs to red ten of diamonds
gaining some peace for my booby-trapped brain
red eight of hearts to a black nine of clubs
lost in chances, black seven to red eight
red six to black seven, black five to six
red four to that five, black three to that four
red two on that three, happy solitaire

43.

Thirty years ago, music was my peace
those happy Walkman cassette playing days
I took some favorite tapes to war with me
like Megadeth's "Peace Sells But Whose Buying"
as well as their new album, "Rust In Peace"
also with me, Ozzy's "Bark At The Moon"
when not on duty, I read, wrote, listened
however, the only song that brought me
back home, far away from that place of war
was not even heavy metal at all
it was Greenwood's "God Bless The USA"
it was on the plane coming home with me
it was everywhere back in that decade
...how'd this song become a racist anthem?

Kenneth Bennight

Kenneth Bennight is a husband, father, lawyer, former Marine, and native Texan. He is the author of the hard-boiled Nacho Perez stories, Nacho Perez, Private Eye and The Truth Shall Make You Dead.

Joyriding The Flyer

Jake banked his F-16 left at Las Vegas and headed north toward Salt Lake City. At 45,000 feet, the deep blue sky floated on a bed of white cumulus clouds.

"Red Rover to Miramar Control. Commencing second leg. Over."

"Miramar Control to Red Rover. Roger that. Out."

Moments later, the radio squawked again. "Damn, Jake. Can you see that?" Karl, Jake's wingman, was to the right and a plane length behind.

"See what."

"On my nose. The damn thing's on my nose."

"What are you talking about?"

Jake dropped just enough airspeed to let Karl pass. A pulsating, diaphanous sphere flew just off Karl's nose.

Jake gasped. "What the hell?"

Karl banked right. The sphere's relative location remained steady. Karl slowed, and the sphere did likewise, synchronized to Karl's maneuvers.

"Remember in *Die Hard* when Bruce Willis says 'Yippee ki yay?'" Karl called.

"Yeah, and?"

"Yippee ki yay."

Karl hit the afterburners and passed Mach 1. The sphere maintained perfect relative position. After a moment, Karl dropped his speed to resume position relative to Jake. The sphere remained on Karl's nose.

The clouds broke, revealing snow-capped mountains below. The sphere left station, descending.

"I'll show the bastard." Karl locked his targeting radar on the sphere.

"Karl, don't do anything stupid."

"This has got to be the ChiComs, and they got no business here. Launch-button cover cleared."

At that instant, almost faster than Karl's eyes could register, the sphere shot upwards. Before he could bring his craft around to follow, the sphere disappeared into the heavens.

"Well, it didn't like that," Karl said.

"You dumb SOB, that wasn't Chicoms. You going to put in your report that you nearly shot down a UFO?"

"I didn't nearly do anything. That sucker could've outrun a missile."

***

Yarnak slammed open the hatch to Lensur's chamber. "What did you do to the flyer, youngling?"

Lensur jolted awake. He poked his eye stalk out of his sleeping gear.

Yarnak could see Lensur's eye stalk try to focus. The confused look on his face betrayed jumbling thoughts, probably none coherent.

"What do you mean?"

"What do you think I mean? And it's high time you were up anyway. It's been four periods since light."

Lensur twitched. "That late? Really? It feels earlier."

"It's not. The flyer. What did you do?"

Lensur swung four of his appendages to the deck and rubbed his carapace. "I don't know. Nothing, really."

"Nothing really? The transmission is cracked, the torque converter's on its last legs. The fuel supply is nearly exhausted. And you did nothing? You think I'll believe that?"

The youngling waved the two appendages not on the deck. "Maybe they were about to go anyway."

"Herbigrazer cud. The flyer was overhauled only two cycles ago. It should be good for 100 cycles. And even then, you don't see that kind of damage."

Yarnak's eye stalk throbbed and pointed directly at him. Lensur squirmed but remained silent. Yarnak snorted. What could the worthless one say?

"You know the flyer belongs to the company? Even though I'll pay for this, I'll still get an unfavorable data note. All because of a youngling with no self-control." Yarnak's eye stalk turned red and his top two appendages bounced.

The youngling squirmed again.

"You were trying to impress a female, weren't you?"

"No, First Parent. We just went for ride, you know. Nothing much."

"Where did you go?"

Lensur shuffled his appendages and squeezed his eye stalk. "It was just this planet, you know. Nothing special."

"No, I don't know. Which planet?"

He retrieved the designation from the implanted chip. "You know, in the MWG78650 System, Sector ZBXG."

Yarnak accessed his own memory chip, and his top appendages spread out and his eye stalk rose vertically to its maximum height. "There? You went there knowing it's forbidden?" He pounded his top two appendages on his carapace. "You went to the third planet, didn't you? You stubborn, insolent, disobedient, unreliable excuse for . . .." His voice trailed off as switched to pounding against the bulkhead.

He paused and breathed deeply. Continuing in a softer voice, he said "I saw reports the authorities know of an intrusion, and they're trying to trace who it was. When I take the flyer in for repairs and refueling, it'll be flagged. I'll have to account for the fuel usage."

He slumped against the bulkhead for several moments. Then he stood erect, eye stalk elevated.

"How did you do the damage?"

"They were going to shoot at me."

"Who? Why?" Yarnak asked.

"I was just surfing their craft's bow wave. Automated control. No risk."

"Except the risk they'll be scared and shoot."

"It's not my fault they're primitive."

"It's your fault you went."

Lensur raised his appendages. "You know, it's not like we took a captive or probed anybody. It was just a little harmless sightseeing. No big deal."

The throbbing in Yarnak's eyestalk intensified, and the stalk itself flashed colors like a parthwah in rut.

More squirming by Lensur.

"Alright, tell me the name of the female. Her parents need to be warned before the authorities come for her.

Lensur's eye stalk pulled back. "Can't we just tell them I was alone. They don't need to know anything else."

"They're not stupid, youngling, and they'll talk to your friends. What's her name?"

Everything on Lensur drooped. "Rishura."

Yarnak took long deep breath and held it before exhaling. "Rishura? My boss's daughter, Rishura? Duchess Rishura? Rishura who's betrothed to the crown prince? That Rishura?"

Lensur's appendages waggled affirmatively.

Yarnak clasped his top two appendages together, his eye stalk wilting. "You've disgraced me at work. You've disgraced me in society. You've committed a prison offense. And now you're telling me you dragged into your criminal scheme a member of the nobility who is also my boss's daughter, one who is betrothed to royalty? You could not possibly have made this worse."

Lensur's eye stalk moved in a circle. "Well, Rishura discovered she's carrying my hatchlings. So I guess she'll lay them in prison."

Yarnak discorporated.

Kristi Sprinkle

Born and raised a writer from Corpus Christi, K now lives on a boat in League City and plans to sail the Intracoastal. She has a ton of words inside and continues to use them—sometimes to poetic effect. But oh! The sea! She has found a vastness that changes all the notions of her past and future.

Ere I seem malapert

Ere I seem malapert,a gnashbag, or even a sciolist, I contend that the puissant scoundrels of this country, led by a growing number of cumbergrounds, have truly made this pestilent malison cause most to see that our nation is saddled with picaroons, fopdoodles, leasing-mongers, dalcops and a gowpen-o' mummers.
The rest of us are thole with wanion, even the sluberdegullions and the roiderbanks. I have, however, not developed lethophobia - yet.

visible briefly

visible briefly Is
A lone metal chair Inside a grove of California trees
Just under a turnpike
(Noticed from a higher road on our way elsewhere)
It sits facing railroad tracks that, from
The chair's eyes, run north and south and disappear in both directions
And I wonder whether a young soul
Or an old soul sits there
And why

Sister Lou Ella Hickman, I.W.B.S.

Sister Lou Ella Hickman's poems and articles have appeared in numerous magazines and journals as well as four anthologies. She was nominated for the Pushcart Prize in 2017 and in 2020. Her first book of poetry entitled *she: robed and wordless* was published in 2015. (Press 53)

eve, for mother's day

how ironic that you were named
mother of all the living . . .
  no parent taught you
   what a woman should be or need:
you had to find your own way
in learning to deal with a man, sons and death
as you also responded to daily bleak mysteries
and moments of little joys
then   did this living make you wise
that bit by bit
you savored the taste of memory
on which you chewed

the spinster

the moon
is an old woman who empties her
purse
    she measures out her change
o
  so carefully
as she counts her coins
  for   each   dark   night

sleeping beauty: the kiss

True love's kiss? . . . I cursed her that way because there is no such thing . . . Sweet Aurora, you stole what was left of my heart. And now I have lost you forever . . .

The character Maleficent in the movie of the same name.

sweet aurora,
would that my sorrow's kiss
wake you from your endless sleep
for you loved me
once a upon a time
as only a child can love
now   my curse
haunts   hunts me . . .
and how i long to ease my jagged pain
yet such agony i will have to bear
should this kiss fail
so
with wounded tenderness
my lips touch your young forehead
to take back the curse
of your forever darkness

Mandy Ashcraft

Mandy is a Doctor of Psychology student specializing in clinical psychology, and a case manager at the Nueces Center for Mental Health and Intellectual Disabilities. She lives in Corpus Christi with her husband Dustin and chihuahua Candy. She has one full-length YA science fiction novel "Small Orange Fruit" available on Amazon, and has been featured annually in the anthology since 2019. This short piece is a statement on perspective.

Two Lanes

Myra's inner voice made its way into the driver's seat. "What is *wrong* with people?" was pressed through gritted teeth. She hit the brakes. She watched a truck, a red truck with a flag swinging from the rearview mirror, transforming traffic into some high-speed obstacle course. Its obstacles were people like her; the recklessness felt personal, as if her life mattered less and that swinging flag and red paint were willing to risk whatever she had to offer the world. Which honestly wasn't much. Did that matter? The at-times subliminal, itching question mark that punctuates all of life's purported meanings left her wondering if maybe the truck was right. Maybe the red paint knew it. Maybe the flag swung to mock her, because what *did* she have to offer? She eased up on the brakes and the rearview mirror clawed at her eyes with sharp reflections of the truck's rectangular taillights. It was almost out of sight. It didn't even care. She wondered what made a person so thoughtless, so careless. Who didn't love them? Who didn't teach them? Then again, who loved her? She hated them because it was possible they were loved more, and that red paint was screaming through traffic about how nice it was to be loved. She resented the behavior because it wasn't about her, and yet somehow it was. Myra could no longer see the truck, and the truck never knew she was there at all.

***

Joshua couldn't breathe. Any sort of sympathetic signal to take a breath, to want—to need—oxygen was hanging in some purgatory of ellipses as his brain struggled to remember how to stay alive. The call said his wife had gone into labor. Their son was moments away from taking his own breath, except it was the kind that turns a fetus into an infant. You only get one of those per lifetime. The stupid flag swung from his rearview mirror in only the wrong places, almost exclusively, but his wife put it there and she loved it. His wife who was having his child. His child who would scream into a fatherless room at any second, because his father was high. High again. He was high again, alone again, lost again, down a dark hallway with one swinging lightbulb that was his unborn son. Until that son wasn't unborn anymore. He was being born, partially born, becoming a newborn, and Joshua knew the clock was rapidly ticking on the semantics. What a devastating paradox afforded to the human condition—to be able to be so high at one's own personal rock bottom. Joshua gripped the wheel and checked his phone; the flat affect of a blank screen gazed up at him in disappointment. It did not blink in text messages or missed calls. *No there are no notifications, because you should've been there. But you weren't. Because you were high.* He pressed the gas. The cars blurred around him like watercolors bleeding into the multicolored scribbles of a sunset. The hospital sign hovered in the distance, providing a target for the cherry-red torpedo he had aimed at the tiny human who awaited his arrival. Or maybe it didn't.

***

"Pull over, there's an ambulance." Eli motioned to the teenager in charge of the wheel and his life for the time being His son was learning to drive, and the colorful fanfare of lights and sounds that announce mortality crept past their vehicle. It was intimidating to Eli's son, as most new things are. The routines and procedures life necessitates are intermittently stapled to a blank handbook in this way; the siren trailed off as the teenager looked at his father for permission to resume normalcy. The car slid back into the lane and Eli glanced sideways at the ambulance that had pulled up to a nursing home. The creeping, twisted spines of distress sting the consciousness when faced with emotions too-often suppressed. The ambulance was not there for his parents and Eli knew this. The nursing center was not even their home. And yet, the car window framed a scene that projected a lifelong fear. He was there with his son, and the evening was beautiful. A gold star in their record of father/son dyadic involvement; this was quality time. The ambulance was parked at the doorway of what was potentially the worst day of someone's life, and for sharp contrast, Eli was having a rather enjoyable evening with his son in plain view of it all. He wished he hadn't noticed it, had just let the sirens sink into unconscious quicksand. The ambulance picked up a stranger to himself, and when it was his parents, they would be strangers to the passers-by. They would be the background noise. And when his son watched the blue and red lights paint his own body, he would be background noise, too. He would be vitally important and utterly insignificant in the same moment. It was almost peaceful to imagine; the full magnitude of primitive and evolutionary fears are distributed into countless perspectives at once. Humanity is necessarily fractured to become whole. It managed to terrify, sadden, and comfort him at the same time. His son laughed at something on the radio and the background noise was silenced.

***

The red truck again. She knew it when she saw it. Myra had turned around, given up on the day, and the evening had snuffed out the last flaming tendril of sunlight. She stood at a gas pump, shoveling that month's retirement check into pump four. She saw the flag, still swinging, but slower. It rocked as it neared her. She felt prickly. "Ma'am," said a man's voice from the window. "Do you know where I can buy an Icee?" An *Icee*. She pondered the word as if it and the individual asking were conceptually mismatched. She met the eyes that guided the question to her face, and his face was not at all what she'd expected. Kind eyes. Strangely innocent features. Soft skin. In her memory he was a miserable, bear-like creature who cackled at the life he neglected to consider around him. "My wife had a baby today. I barely made it in time, but I made it. She said the only thing she wanted was an Icee." Myra motioned toward the station. She followed him inside and poured herself an Icee, too. It wasn't half bad; a frozen, macerated cloud of sugar with a straw. "New dad, huh?" she said. He nodded and paid for both. The way she studied him made him wonder if he knew her, or if she knew him somehow. She looked at him as if she'd known him somewhere else, maybe even a dream. A middle-aged man stood behind them with his teenage son, and the man offered a somewhat timeless piece of advice to the new parent: "Good luck." They laughed as Eli tugged at the boy's shirt sleeve. There were no other words exchanged. They would never cross paths again and didn't need to. In that otherwise unremarkable moment they were different and alike, broken and whole, old and new, jotted down mindlessly onto the same torn sheet of time like a note that would be lost or thrown away. Myra would go home to a message about an ambulance call she'd forgotten how much she feared. Through muddied thoughts about being unloved, she had lost sight of the people who always had. The empty Icee cup would stand on her counter for weeks like a damp, cherry-flavored time capsule. Eli's son would learn that his favorite teacher had just given birth to a baby boy. That teacher would spend the next few weeks sipping Icees while he slept. Jonathan would relapse and find himself under blue and red lights that would save his life; the same lights that haunted Myra and Eli for reasons that were not so much dissimilar as occurring at points on a timeline so far apart that they failed to realize there was only ever one line. It really never mattered that they'd crossed paths at all. Except that it did.

Manuel Ruiz

Manuel Ruiz is a life-long Texan with a passion for reading, video games and music. He works in IT, plays in an 80's band, and owns way too many toys. He writes teen and adult fiction, usually with a supernatural twist, and loves to keep his readers on their toes. His novel *The Sugar Skull* is about 17-year-old Ricky Luna, who wants nothing more than to finish school, win the hand of his best girl, and get away from his troubling home life. Then there is a midnight visit from a strange young girl.

Excerpt from ***The Sugar Skull***

"What is it, Grandma Bea?"

"I went to see a few friends from the neighborhood. I covered almost ten houses across three different streets over seven blocks. Three different people saw or talked to that little girl last night. And those were just the ones that wanted to admit it."

"They saw her, too?"

"Yes, some did. Mrs. Blackmon down the street said that she also heard the little girl chasing after her cat, but it was Janie that had the best information."

"The nosy one that's always asking about Mom?"

"Yes, that one. Well, her nosiness helped for once. She asked the little girl where she lived like I did, but after she pointed and told her, Janie kept pressing her. She asked her where exactly. She told her on Creek Street on the corner."

"That's like three streets down, right?"

"Yes. So this morning, Janie went down to that street because it sounded familiar to her. She went to the house and saw what was left of it. In all the years we've lived in this neighborhood, that place where her house sits has always been empty and just seems like it's an extended side yard. Janie said there's a foundation slab, but it's covered in grass."

"So there's nothing but a slab?" Ricky asked. "Was there ever a house there?"

"This is where her nosiness goes to another level. She went to the Stone Creek County Clerk's office to get the property history and found out the last residents there were a family named Seger. They were a married couple that lived there over thirty years ago with four kids, and one night the house caught fire. They all got out, but one of their daughters ran back in looking for her cat. Her parents rushed in after her and the house collapsed. The three of them were killed, leaving three orphans behind. The house was never rebuilt since no one wanted to build there after finding out such a horrible tragedy had occurred, so the city decided to maintain ownership and leave the lot empty."

"Are you sure it was that little girl?"

"Janie got a record of the incident and showed me a copy. The little girl loved to play in her small plastic pool and wore her bathing suit to bed sometimes. She was wearing it that night and when they found her body, she was holding her cat. Its name was Kitty."

"Are you saying," Freddy said, his voice rising, "that we talked to a ghost?"

"It seems it's at least possible that happened," Bea answered without hesitation.

"I think I'm going to be sick," Freddy said.

Ricky was struck silent for a few seconds before his face lit up.

"Are you kidding? That's one of the coolest things that's ever happened. We saw a ghost! If she would have tried to kill us or looked like Freddy Krueger, then okay, that's not cool and I'd be terrified, but come on! How many people can say they saw and talked to a ghost?"

Freddy half smiled. "I guess you're right, but I still feel like I might pass out."

A look of concern came over Ricky's face. "Grandma, so has she been haunting this place all this time? I mean, has anyone else seen her before last night?"

"That's what's strange," Grandma said. "No. I've lived here so long and know most of the neighbors on the next few streets, but I've never heard about her before. If a spirit had been haunting this area, you'd think someone would have said something or seen something long ago."

"So, why now?"

Grandma Bea shook her head. "I don't know, but that same question has me worried."

"Worried about what?" Ricky asked.

"If that girl appeared to so many people last night, she had to have a reason. It's not a good sign. A spirit usually wanders because it died suddenly or has unfinished business. She did die in a tragedy, but as far as we know, she's never been seen before and that makes me think she was here for a completely different reason. From what the neighbors said, it sounds like she was looking for something more than her Kitty."

It's About Healing by Cynthia Alvarez

Mariah Massengill

Mariah Massengill is a coastal bend native who recently completed her Master of Fine Arts in Creative Writing from the University of Houston-Victoria. Currently, Mariah uses her love for prose and poetry in her field of theatre, where she enjoys writing, translating, and adapting plays. Her one act plays have been featured in competitive readings by Berg Originals and Actor's Lab RGV. Her play *Green* was produced as part of Rialto Theatre's 2021 Twenty-Four Hour Playfest. She is excited to begin working on her doctorate in Asian Theatre at the University of Hawaii at Manoa this fall.

An instructor once posed a question to one of my classes, "If you died tomorrow, what would your epitaph say?" How do you fit the body of a life on a headstone? I realized during this exercise that my epitaph if I died as an infant, at 16, 22, 40, or the ripe age of 100 would all be irreconcilably different. The poems wouldn't seem to resemble the same life. So I've decided to chronicle my life through epitaphs. If I die tomorrow from the day I drafted this, remember me by this epitaph, 28.

28

They called the wind Mariah.

The smooth roundness of her face prepared her to take criticism,
rolling downhill, a wheel accelerating to reckless self-destruction.

She looked for kinship by flipping rocks—
grabbing more than she could carry
before they scurried away—
as they always did, by grip of death or some escape
more personal.

Lacking from the beginning, she tried to invent worth,
but like dirt, it slipped through her fingers—
Always out of her element.

To Be, or Used to Be...

This decrepit monster house used to be
a suite of youth and dreams
until momma heard strangers shouting in the attic
and she drowned us in her screams

This soulless zombie used to be
a nurturing heart to all my woes
until she heard radios buzzing in the air
and even her family became foes

This humid hell-spa used to be
a bath of tranquility and vanilla spice
until momma heard Satan thrusting in the bubbles
and she gave birth to the platypus Antichrist

This Franken-family used to be
a system that dysfunctioned together
until her doctor missed cancer throbbing in the madness
and her neck fell limp with the peeling skin of old leather

This rattling whisper used to be
a belter of both endearing and dated tunes
until momma heard Death humming in the corner
and we walked her down his aisle with fanfare of bassoons

Matthew Rosas

Matt Rosas is the author of *The Legend of Mariquita and other Short Stories*, and of the upcoming novella, *Praying not to Fall.* Matt's short story, "The Angel," was featured in *The Bilingual Review of Arizona State University.* He studied Short Fiction and Flash Fiction with Inprint, Inc.

If Wishes Were Horses

My grandmother cooked every night. Picadillo, Fideo, enchiladas, caldo, arroz con pollo, rice, beans, and pot roast on Sundays with potatoes and carrots in the pot. She loved cooking for family. But, once a month, she'd get tired and we'd have Boat n' Net and she'd enjoy every bite of it. Fried shrimp or fried fish and a yummy squishy biscuit for less than five bucks. And, the best tartar sauce in town. You'd do the Walk-up window to eat there at a scruffy picnic table with seagulls staring at you, or you'd take it home in the colorful box.

Her son, my dad, hated seafood. But, he'd love to cook it. He'd cook up fried fish, and even better, seafood gumbo on white rice with fresh boiled crab, oysters, and okra. He never ate a bite himself, just loved to make it for all. My older brother, usually caught most of the fish and crabs and sometimes even the fresh-shucked oysters. His fishing skills grew polished with age, and he'd cast a throw net with effortless ease I could never manage.

His surfing skills were average, but still better than mine. I miss the day trips we'd take. Load up the suburban with our boards, pick up our friend Celis, stop at Dockside for wax, and hit the beach near Bob Hall. Celis had a quad fin, Butch a tri, and mine was a single fin Surfboards Hawaii bought used with dings. It was there we learned to surf, shared our first joint, and savored that ice cold coke in a Styrofoam cup from the pier snack shop. On the drive back, we'd pass by Dockside, sometimes stopping for a sticker, drop off Celis, and hose down the boards.

In our room, he'd crank up the radio playing "Wishes" by Jon Butcher on the Sea 101 Corpus Christi Rocks, and close his eyes and sing the words. Once darkness set, the paper plates of gumbo were brought to the table and we sat with smiles that now at this second I tear up wanting to be there again in Corpus at Boat n' Net with Butch, not gone, and grandma waiting for us at our childhood home, not worrying about cooking for just one night.

Mulberry-34

Mulberry-34 is a lifelong Adventurer who writes under a nom de plume.

Adventure #*6244*

As a songbird chirps in the distance, I gather my belongings and prepare to begin my journey. Being sure to bring an ample water supply, binoculars, proper clothing, and my trusty knife, I feel confident in my carry-on. The distinctive call of a mockingbird, signals the start of the journey. I am on the northernmost tip of the Oso Bay Wetlands Preserve. The beautiful and majestic cumulus clouds take up the southern sky. Crossing over the stream that acts as a barrier between city and nature, I am on a mission in search of the northern caracara, a bird of prey that resides here in South Texas. Immediately, I see a lonely cottontail rabbit scurrying upon the notice of my presence. Curious about what lies ahead, I trek deeper into the woods. Mother Nature has her way of entrancing the mind and I completely forget that the city is only a stone's throw behind me. Finally, I come to a shallow pond filled with minnows, turtles, and ducks playing in cool green water. What a wonderful thing to experience this hidden side of nature. I have become entirely immersed in its beauty. Spending roughly 10 minutes at this location, I find that it is time to move on and continue the mission of getting a glimpse of a northern caracara. Situated high in an old mesquite tree is a large, grayish ball the size of a basketball that appears to be made of mud. It is some kind of wasp nest, so I move on towards something not so dangerous. I take notice of a few house sparrows, mockingbirds, and doves. After an extensive search, I have not spotted the northern caracara and it is now time to head back. It has been an unforgettable trip. I have gotten to see things that I would otherwise not have seen being chained to the conveniences of modern life. Although I did not accomplish the goal of spotting a northern caracara, I have been successful in other areas. I have sharpened my observation skills and learned to pay attention to the subtle things in life, like the call a mockingbird makes when it warns other birds that there is a predator in the area. This is a day to be remembered and hopefully one to be repeated. After all, I still have to spot that northern caracara!

Michelle Eccellente Stevenson

Michelle Eccellente Stevenson is a mom, wife, abstract artist, writer, TEDx Speaker, and Founder of Cultivate Caring. The bulk of Michelle's career was spent in the training and development sector, working for major corporations as an educator. She now spends her time trying to make sense of the world through art and writing. Color and mood define her visual art pieces and themes of humanity bind Michelle's literary works. She invites you to join her on social media @CultivateCaring and @MESStudioArt.

Slicing Away

Yesterday, I met my
Crushing hate

Playing a game of peek-a-boo
In no way resembling
Childhood fun

Deft he was,
Slicing away pieces of me
Attentively extracting
Layer after layer
To nourish the one I hate
Leaving me with
Nothing

Now standing before me
Introducing itself
With toxic clarity

My hate became too heavy

In the Beginning

Blood
Sweat
Tears

Blood from the womb
That is no longer needed

Sweat from my mother's toil

Tears from us and them

Pain, confusion, joy

Born into this world
Flash of bright light
Cold dry air

Where am I?

Take me back to
That soothing
Lub-dub, lub-dub, lub-dub

Strange noises
Thrown into chaos

Taken away from
My everything

Mike Mercer

Mike Mercer's experimental novel *Forever Alone* chronicles the character's odyssey from Vietnam to West Texas to Mexico and finally to an unexpected reunion with a Vietnam Veteran. His upcoming novel Cantina Azul is set mostly in Ajajic, Mexico

An excerpt from **Cantina Azul**

Afternoon Wednesday June 18, 2003
Ajajic, Mexico

Think the first time I entered The Blue Tequila Cantina was six years ago. Mexican natives call it Cantina Azul. They say a Gringo named Tom opened this bar in 1987 and still lives within even though he passed on in 1996. It must be true as sometimes I get messages from Tom relating to something is going to happen or when someone is coming. Sometimes I know the name of who is coming. Easy says, I spook her when I forecast someone, or something, is coming round the corner. Kinda surprises me too, but then I've not had a normal lifetime. Spent more time sitting at this end of the bar than any one place in my sixty- three years. Easy has been here three and a half, and we have seen it all, fun, terror, blessing, and wonderful memories.

Some things you need to know: Easy is not the bartender's name, but she is quite easy on the eyes, not sure of her real name, or where she is from. My place at the end of the bar is my long-standing, pen-in-hand, writing comfort zone. Somedays, I go home and write sober and coherent. Leigh, yes Leigh, the one stable strong good woman in my life I do not deserve, watches over me as the angel she is.

The Blue Tequila Cantina serves as a meeting place for expats from over the world. Some seeking, love, some seeking companionship, some enjoying a cheap lifestyle, oh and some escaping their past. All told, a good bunch of people, using up the end of life as we know it. Brave people, taking a chance on something different. The locals carry us high, we appreciate all the services they provide. Many frequent the bar and most local closings on property sales are finalized in the Cantina Azul. Oh yes, this is the local NASCAR TV headquarters. All Mexicans drive too fast, when you ask them why, they say we are in training for NASCAR.

And just like that, it happened again today. Normally, folks frequenting the bar don't ask questions of each other as we all have something we don't want to talk about. So, we find out about each other by what they say, not by prying.

Extending his hand, he says, "My name is Sid, may I sit the bar with you?"

"Sure Sid, my name is Jerry, we've been expecting you." I replied.

"How do you know me. I have never been here before?" A surprised, Sid remarks.

"A few days ago, a gust of wind blew a crumpled piece of paper in the door. I knew it was for me, when I spread the paper out it had 'Sid' printed on it."

"Ah, I don't believe it for a minute!" Sid said.

"Easy, come, aqui," I call.

Easy approaches and says, "yo is Sid esta so?"

Not believing what he is experiencing Sid says, "I need a beer!"

"Easy bring Sid a Tecate, make that dos since Sid is buying.

"Sid, in here 'yo' means, hi, you, me, a cheer, or an explanation point. Always say 'yo' when you answer the phone. Just how it is," I advised as Easy fishes deep in the cooler for the Tecate. "What you need, Sid, maybe we can help."

"I been walking these streets a couple of months checking out the area. Kinda thinking I might move to Ajajic. I'm too young to retire and thought I might try buying this bar."

"I laughed out loud, Easy chimed in with a beautiful smile. In fact, I laughed so hard and long I broke into a violent coughing spell, ending with sweat and wheezing."

Meanwhile Sid sipped his beer and waits for things to settle down, "you OK Jerry?"

"Think so, but I think Tom is tellin' me to warn you off."

"Who is Tom, and why should I be concerned with Tom?"

"Tom owns the bar, Sid, what makes it concerning is he has been dead since 1996. Easy runs the place, opens, and closes the Cantina, and sometime in the night the till is collected, money and directions left to pay various vendors. More than 3 years ago, before Easy, the guy running the bar tried to sell it to a newcomer. Both ended up missing and the police closed the bar.

"It was hard on me, as this was, as this is, my away from home, home. Couple of months later I dropped by, behold Easy had the door open for business. I ask her what happened. She put finger to lips and then waved it at me. I knew to just drop it, and be happy. So be careful about trying to buy the Cantina."

Mona Schroeder

Mona Schroeder is a writer and former librarian who lives in Corpus Christi, Texas.

The Tree Doctor

The tree is hemorrhaging sap, black against the gray bark, the leaves still green but washed out, lackluster. I know nothing about trees. A city girl, born and raised, I've always viewed trees as curiosities, like zoo animals. This is the first tree I've ever owned. It came with the house, also a first. I have property now, a mortgage, and a sickly tree.

Should I put a bucket beneath? A bandage? A yellow ribbon? I'm lost.

My next-door neighbor, Earl, ambles over, a beer in his hand. Earl is retired. In the afternoons he likes to enthrone himself in the lawn chair that he keeps in his garage. He leaves the garage door up, so he can watch the world go by while slugging back a beer or two – or three. Occasionally Earl favors a neighbor with sage advice, as he does now to me.

"You know what you otter do?" Earl says, swigging.

Otter do? Oh, ought to do, I realize. Sometimes Earl requires translation. "What's that, Earl?" I ask, warily. I'm protective of the tree all of a sudden, worried that he'll say have it removed, a bad omen, and something I've been worried about.

"Call one of those tree people to take a look-see." Swig.

"Tree people?"

"Yeah, you know, tree people." Swig, swig.

Later, I look up tree care online, skipping over the ones for tree removal, and find a name that strikes my fancy. The Tree Doctor. Must I call him Doctor Tree? Maybe I'll ask to see his arborist credentials first. Or perhaps I'll ask him about that tree falling in a forest thing. I've always wondered about that.

When Dr. Tree arrives, he's wearing ordinary clothes – khakis and a blue polo shirt. No white coat, which is slightly disappointing. He's about my age, mid-thirties, with an earnest look – or perhaps it's the clipboard which lends him an official air. Together we examine the ailing tree.

"It came with the house," I explain, so that he doesn't blame me for the tree's condition. Irresponsible tree owner, committing a crime against nature. I will not be labeled a tree murderer unjustly!

He launches into a diagnosis of the tree's condition, which frankly I only half listen to – something about it's the wrong type of tree for this area (again, not my fault), recommends a series of treatments to help revive the tree, although there's no guarantee, etc., etc. Then he hands me his business card, which seems wrong somehow. He's giving me a card made from his own patients? Who's the tree murderer now?

"Well, thanks for coming by," I say. "I'll give you a call when I've decided."

"Sure thing," Dr. Tree says. "Just don't wait too long. She's in distress right now. I can give her a treatment before I leave. That'll help some. Of course, she won't be out of the woods yet," he drawls, straight-faced.

She? Not out of the woods? I like his tree-side manner. "You're hired," I say.

Neesy Tompkins

Neesy Tompkins is a writer and photographer. She lives in Port Aransas and often writes about the area

The Salty Dog

When Rhonda first opened The Salty Dog Saloon, she and partner Larry had just moved from Austin after owning a few honky tonks there in Manchaca and South Austin.

Their roots were true to Texas but they wanted an Island Bar with a Texas flair in the town they wished to settle in, the town they fell in love with.

A saddle perched high above the bar, Gene Autry photographs adorned its walls and an old fashioned coin jukebox filled with old honky tonk favorites provided a backbone for a true Texas honky tonk that somehow managed to keep its Austin roots while maintaining a good solid local base of regulars. Way before it became known as a karaoke bar, you'd find the bartender scattering corn meal on the old wood dance floor, keeping it slick for boot scooters. On any given night, you'd see both two steppers in boots right alongside flip-flopped and sandy feet. And the perfect branding of its signature drink, the Salty Dog added a tropical twist with the large wedge of Texas grown grapefruit perched perfectly onto a frozen mug adorned with salted rim filled with ice, gin and grapefruit juice. Back in the day, Salty Dogs went for $2.50 day or night and Rhonda kept them affordable even for the locals in winter when times were slim.

In the mid 90's, Steve Coughman was the gravelly voice of Texas Radio. His legacy remains as he urged Texans to support Texas music. And that Rhonda did. Rhonda incorporated well known favorite blues acts, the likes of Rocky Benton, Dicky Neely, Triggerfish and even Austinites Shelly King and Rosie Flores in the early days that packed the house. By keeping local bands working and that cold beer coming, the Salty Dog established a name for itself in an old building that had been renamed several times and seen several owners come and go.

When asked one day what type of slogan should go on the outside sign, it only seemed fitting to employ the old adage of Steve Coughman by incorporating his constant referral of Port Aransas as the Texas Riviera into "Coolest Honky Tonk on the Texas Riviera".

And there you have it. And there it is.

And on this the eve of the Grand Opening of Rhonda's Salty Dog Saloon, all hats are tipped towards the lady as the Salty Dog Saloon reopens in a grand sort of way on this the eve of the 2 year anniversary since Harvey.

It stirs a sense of pride and relief that the portion of town which lay dormant and dark for so long, will be filled once again with light and music and laughter.

Through hell and high water, The Salty Dog Saloon is back. Long may she reign as "Coolest Honky Tonk on the Texas Riviera

Nolan Read

Written by Nolan K. Read upon receiving a letter regarding a visit by his son and his wife in 1996. Nolan passed away on Oct. 26, 2019. His wife, Esther, submitted this.

Dear Son,

You have exaggerated the anticipated crowded conditions. There should be no real concern of crowded conditions except when we use the restroom, bathe, eat, watch TV, and sleep. You forgot the hidden bed in the den and the hidden backpacks in the hallway closet.

Your wife and you can use Maria's room. Mark and Maria can use our room. The boys can use Matt's room, and you can use the den (except when we are watching TV.) We also have a sofa-bed in the garage; however, there is not room in the garage to unfold it. You could use that couch outside if it does not rain. I do not think it will rain.

We are in a severe drought condition. Emergency measures are now in force. Our lakes are 2/3rds empty with no significant rain predicted. Residential users are advised to bathe instead of showering. We will allow ½" of water in the bathtub per bather with baths limited to one per person per day. We do expect you to save this water and pour it on the lawn.

If you shower, you must wet yourself first and then turn it off. After lathering, then turn on to rinse quickly and turn off. You may wonder how you are going to recoup such little water. Simple. After drying throw your towel into the bathtub and hand squeeze into a plastic pail. You will use a glass to brush your teeth. You will determine other water conservation measures as you proceed.

We are limited to watering the yard to one day a week, Tuesdays for us. We must water by hand. You take the front yard and your wife can take the back yard. There is no watering of the yard allowed on weekends and no watering allowed on any weekday between 10:00 am and 6:00 pm.

Yes, we had a very mild winter, which is to say, almost no winter at all. As a result, we have an epidemic of roaches. It's not the little ones; it's the big ones. The roaches did not die off this winter; instead, they kept growing. These are humongous roaches. Boric acid tablets can't kill them. And, they are really fast. Raid kills them on direct contact. As a result, you find yourself in all sorts of positions attempting to make direct contact. Good aim and a fast reaction is a must.

Your mother and I returned home last Saturday at midnight. A dozen fleas jumped her. This is the first problem of fleas we have had since the dogs were bathed about a week ago. We had not seen a single flea since that time. The moral to this story is that you don't have to worry about finding the fleas; the fleas will find you.

Believe it or not, our first line of defense is the dogs. Our dogs are kept overnight in the utility room. As the roaches run in at all times of the night underneath the rear door, they are met head on by the dogs (who hate the roaches as much as you will.) The dogs bark and pursue the roaches with vigor. As a matter of fact, I picked up several dead ones this morning in the utility room.

Our dogs will probably bark at you. But when they lick your hand or face remember, these dogs are your first line of defense. Without them you will probably be spraying all night long.

It's really going to be nice to have several extra hands join us in this war. Be sure to bring several cans of Raid. Don't leave home without it.

Love, Mom and Dad

Norman C. Delaney, PhD

Norman Delaney taught history for many years at Del Mar College.

Writing History with Integrity

During my years of teaching and researching history, I have had to deal with a lot of bad writing along with the good. It is all too easy to be fooled. One such occasion occurred on February 2, 1970. William Red Fox's *Memoirs of Chief Red Fox* had recently been published by McGraw-Hill at a time of renewed interest in Native American history and the book subsequently became a best seller.

It tells of how at the age of six Red Fox (not to be confused with comedian Redd Foxx) had been at Little Big Horn on that fateful day, June 25, 1876, when Lieutenant Colonel George Armstrong Custer and five companies of his Seventh Cavalry were wiped out by Sioux and Cheyenne warriors. As a young man he performed with Buffalo Bill's Wild West show. Now a celebrity, Red Fox was appearing regularly on *The Johnny Carson Show*, usually with Bob Hope, and the two would reminisce about the early years of vaudeville. Red Fox's popularity had brought him speaking engagements at both Harvard and Oxford. I took a chance and phoned Mr. Red Fox and asked if he would speak to one of my history classes at Del Mar College and he agreed. I was thrilled at the prospect of having my students meet a man who represented "living history." When I picked up Mr. Red Fox at the apartment complex where he lived by himself, he was garbed in the impressive regalia of an Oglala chief. I was amazed at his physical fitness at 102 years of age as he walked briskly beside me. My classroom was packed with students, some from other classes of mine as well. But to my dismay, Red Fox's presentation did not ring true. Many of his facts were simply wrong, such as his reference to Custer's "son," although Custer and his wife Libbie never had any children. I regretted that I had brought him after all.

Not long after his visit, Red Fox's book began unraveling. An investigative reporter discovered that he was not a chief and Oglala tribal leaders in South Dakota had never heard of him. In his book he had given three entirely different locations where he was born. And worst of all, his entire chapter on Wounded Knee had been lifted word for word from a book published in 1940. Red Fox denied all allegations, conceding only that his "chief" designation was an "honorary" title. From my experience with Mr. Red Fox, I learned to be far more cautious in what I exposed my students to.

I am currently writing a biography of John Warren Kittredge (1818–1889), a ship captain and United States naval officer best known for his attack on Corpus Christi in August of 1862. Shortly afterward, Kittredge was captured while ashore at Flour Bluff to obtain buttermilk he had a craving for. In the course of my research, a book on Padre Island turned up that appeared to be well documented and I thought might be useful. It was a collaboration by members of the Writers Round Table of Corpus Christi published in 1950 by the Naylor Company of San Antonio. The book, however, turned out to be a disappointment and no wonder. Here is its reference to Kittredge's capture:

> When [Captain Kittredge] was surprised by one of [Captain John] Ireland's Rangers in the kitchen of a Flour Bluff home, he dashed buttermilk in the Ranger's face and dived for an open window. The Ranger grabbed a trouser leg and held on.
>
> Then the captain [Kittredge] shed both dignity and trousers and raced through the sand—and straight into the Ranger's arms.

This is the kind of baloney that Hollywood refers to as "dramatic license" in its versions of history but has no place in a book purported to be "nonfiction." More recently, the writer of a pseudo-military history of South Texas has made his Kittredge into the champion chess player of the entire fleet complete with dialogue! An historian I admire, Bell Wiley, a stickler for writing true accounts of Civil War soldiers, said it best: "Write history as though the past was peering over your shoulder."

When I researched my first book, *John McIntosh Kell of the Raider* Alabama, I found it necessary to travel to Washington, D.C., and the National Archives there, Atlanta, Georgia, for its archives, and towns in Georgia to interview Kell's grandchildren. When I later researched *The Maltby Brothers' Civil War*, I was able to find much useful information at the Corpus Christi Central Library from microfilm copies of the *Ranchero*, the newspaper published by Henry Maltby in Corpus Christi and later Brownsville. Research on Kittredge has been totally different because of the Internet, which involves much more than merely googling a name and checking genealogical websites. My subject is somewhat of a Jekyll-Hyde whose life has required a great deal of sleuthing. No personal correspondence of his or descendants have turned up, not even a likeness, and the various spellings of his name require a great deal of cross-checking. Although Kittredge's Civil War naval record, including his court-martial, is now obtainable online, libraries and university archives must still be checked out. Persistence has paid off and although some questions still remain unanswered, the information found has been astonishing. My Jekyll/Hyde received a gold medal for saving a child from drowning yet was court-martialed and dismissed from the navy for having brutally beaten one of his sailors. He had a reputation as a competent ship captain before he wrecked a magnificent passenger liner off the coast of southern California, endangering the lives of 500 passengers and crew members. In 1850, when living in Kenosha, Wisconsin, he was elected alderman because of his squeaky-clean reputation, and yet five years later was in Sing Sing prison for having threatened a ship's waiter with a pistol while first mate on board the *St. Louis*. He loved his wife dearly and yet even as she was dying, he was having an extramarital affair that resulted in a child born out of wedlock. Not the kind of a biography that Kittredge would have wanted but all of it true. A biography of John Warren Kittredge has the makings of a winner, and whether or not its author becomes a guest speaker at Harvard and Oxford, it will be written with integrity!

Patterns of Light by Jeff Janko

Patricia Alaniz

Born in Taft, Texas, Patricia Alaniz is the 13th of 14 children. Her love of reading and writing poetry began when she was a teenager. Patricia's poems are inspired by the lives of those she holds dear. She is the author of *Whispers of Love Poetry: Emotions of the Soul.*

Wild Child

She was a wild child!
Conspicuous,
 and vivid!
A true advocate
 of her own chaos!
Entwined by love,
 beauty,
 and rebellion!
A bit vague,
 but self absorbed.
Yes...
 She was indeed
 a beautiful creature!
A true masterpiece…
 Of her own storm
of imperfections!

The Bullies

Please.. Go away!
Just let me play!
Oh Why,
  Must you.. ruin my day?!
Just let me be!
Oh, can't you see?!
The way..
  that they.. make fun of me?!
They took my phone!
I can't go home!
Oh why, won't they..
  leave me alone?!
They push and shove!
I plead.. Enough!!
Praying to God..
  take me above!
I dare not cry.
I only sigh.
Sometimes I feel..
  I'd rather die!
They mock my words.
I'm left unheard.
And still you say..
  it's all absurd!
I beg you please!
I'm on my knees!
Open your eyes..
  and rescue me!

Pete Adler

Originally from West Virginia, Pete Adler has spent the past 49 years in Corpus Christi. He recently emerged from pandemical isolation to travel, play poker and compile his collection of found poems, each line taken from an internet news site headline.

Waiting for the tooth fairy

...for STP

I raise his haggard frame,
my hand at his spine, feeling the ribs press back
through tarpaper skin,
hold the rasp of his lungs in my palm,
each breath the hiss and crackle
of a Lightning Hopkins 78.

unshaved face
cracked and bleeding forearms
the curled, yellow toenails of Howard Hughes.

She dotes, tending to every need with a loving hand
derived from 50 years of sleeping at his side,
crushes the oversized Rx tablet with the back of a spoon
and gingerly ladles the shards into his mouth
then wipes away
the spittle and jetsam from his lower lip.

still
his mouth gapes, unable to close on its own.
doleful eyes shut tight then open with effort,
only to close again in quiet submission.

You lean to touch and give a kiss,
to kiss the lips you have not kissed
since you were just a little girl,
that expression of emotion was never part of your world.
a tear slips down the bridge of your nose

onto his sunken, spotted cheek.
you wish to tell him of your love but
your voice is absent, you cannot speak.

with bowed legs no longer strong enough to carry him
he finds himself placed upon a bedpan
humbled by the fate of 60 years of unfiltered nicotine and tar.
with heavy tongue, he labors to communicate
the confusion
the frustration
the pain

He reaches in slow motion to grab an offered hand,
clutching limply with discolored, impotent fingers.
a cracked-tooth demi-smile lights the entire room
with its unexpected emergence
then disappears too soon.

Cancer, the one-eyed cur, howls in the night.

Paul Aster Cohen

Paul Aster Cohen is a pseudonym for a local writer, filmmaker, photographer and graphic artist.

I Made a Movie Once

Angelo stopped mid-drink and leaned in closer to his laptop screen to make sure he had actually read what he thought he had. He swallowed hard, coughed, then looked over the email again before hitting reply and speedily typed out a response. Before he could think twice, he hit send.

He spun around in his desk chair and raised his fists in victory. Within a few minutes he was tossing piles of old luggage and unworn clothes out of his storage closet looking for a long lost, but not forgotten, friend. After nearly emptying the closet, he emerged with a plastic container, covered in dust with one corner held together with duct tape. An enormous grin rippled across his face.

There was a time, many years ago when that worn old tub was his only companion as he crossed the country from film festivals to comic book conventions and back again, slinging its contents to anyone interested. He set the tub on his coffee table, knocking over some week-old beer bottles.

Childlike giddiness bathed his face as he popped off the grey top and looked inside. Posters, stickers, buttons and finally the objects he was searching for; DVDs still shrink-wrapped and neatly packed in a row, untouched by time. There was a Macabre Monster Fest badge packed in the container, too. That festival had ended his quest. He met a low-level distributor who seemed to show interest at first and then told him his work was amateurish at best.

Angelo flipped the badge over a few times before tossing it in a nearby trash bin and began pulling everything out and setting it neatly on the floor next to him. Excitement was coursing through his eager fingertips. He pored over every piece of swag as if it was new. Memories of making the film washed over him in waves with every whiff of glossy poster and piece of thick, crumpled carboard he would place amongst the table to promote his goods.

Once it was all unpacked, stacked and organized, he slowly lifted one of the DVDs as if it was the Holy Grail and held it up to the light.

"You will have chance in sun once more my dear old friend," he said before laughing to himself at the absurd dramatic tone of his voice.

In another few minutes, he was out of his apartment, nearly

floating down the sidewalk with joy with a large, padded envelope tucked under his arm. With a smile plastered across his face, he waved to passersby who in return tossed him uneasy scowls. They clinched purses, moved aside uneasily but he didn't care. A runaway buss could've plowed over him, but it still wouldn't have brought him down.

At the end of the block he found a mailbox, stared at the envelope like a lover leaving on a jet plane, then pulled down the handle and lay the envelope down. He lifted the handle and heard it land quietly inside. He took a deep breath, taking in nothing but smog-filled air, then continued on his way, pulling his phone from his pocket to call Levi.

"Man, you'll never guess what just happened!" he exclaimed over the line.

The voice answered, "You finally got your shit together, met a girl, you guys are getting married in the fall, there's a baby on the way, if it's a girl you'll name her Joon and if it's a boy you'll name him Levi, after me of course, and you'll play the market, nothing too risky but not too safe either, and make some cash and you two will move out of your crappy apartment, get a house in the suburbs, invite me over for holidays, but I won't come because I'm an asshole, then finally your kids will have kids and you'll get old and die. Before your wife of course, because you're an asshole, too." Silence fell over the line. "Am I close?"

"I just got an email from this film festival I haven't even heard of, and they want to make my movie the main feature! They even plane and hotel reservations for me."

"Wow," Levi said. "I thought what I said was funny, but looks like you take the cake."

"I'm serious! I just sent out the DVD, it's on its way!"

"You're not at all thinking this is a bit weird? Some rando festival wants to feature some little movie you made, what, 10 years ago? My creep factor would be tipping the scales right about now."

"I thought you'd be excited, too? I mean, you helped."

"I helped because you're my friend, not because I have Hollywood aspirations. And besides, I thought you gave all that up."

"I'm excited and I'm flying out there."

Levi paused. "Too bad Kelly won't be there."

Silence fell between the two men.

"Yea, it sucks," Angelo said in a more somber tone. "I'll call her folks and let them know. They'd be happy their daughter is still remembered I think." He had stopped walking and was leaning against a storefront window.

"Yeah. Probably," Levi uttered knowing he probably shouldn't have brought it up. "Look, congrats on the movie thing but I got to go. Take care and holler at me when you get back to tell me all about it."

"Will do. Take care, Levi. Talk to you soon."

Angelo slid the phone back in his pocket and shuffled back home.

The next few weeks were spent chasing down the actors from his film on social media and sending them messages sharing the news. A somber, nagging thought paced around in the back of his head the whole time. It was odd that after so many years, someone was interested in his film.

All the actors blew him off. Some pretended to not even know who he was. Others didn't even respond to his messages.

That didn't keep him from designing new promotional movie posters and getting his old t-shirts reprinted. Every time he worked on the files, he would see Kelly's face adorning the material, and sadness would begin to creep in. He knew it would be the right thing to do if he visited Kelly's parents, but he hadn't seen them since the accident. Well, since after the accident. At the hospital in the waiting room.

Angelo took a long swig of cheap whisky and closed his laptop.

The week of the screening, he was picking up the new posters from a print shop when a fat, hairy man in a wife beater came from the back with a long thin box.

"You're that kid that made that movie, right? This is you?" he said pointing to the box of posters.

Angelo stood taller and grinned.

"Yessir, that's me."

"I heard about you. My boy told me you lived around here, the filmmaker. I remember it was shown over at the theater by that corn dog joint. That the same flick?"

"You got it."

"That was some years back. I went there and saw the thing. It was good. When you gonna make another one? I'd like to see another one."

"You know," he said feeling confident, "Maybe soon. I have some ideas so you never know."

"I can't wait to see whatever you come up with. Just don't make it one of them zombie movies. They got a million of those things." Angelo pulled out one of the posters and begin looking over it as the man peered over the counter. "And that girl, there on the front, where it says 'Dedicated to so and so', she died right? I think I read it in the papers."

Angelo slid the poster back in the box.

"Yeah. She did."

"Frickin' shame, man. She was so good in that movie. I felt like she was really scared. Like, for reals. She was a good dame. Died in a car wreck or something, right?"

Angelo passed the man his debit card.

"Something like that."

"It's on the house, lil' buddy," the man said passing the debit card back. "It ain't every day we get famous dudes in here. Dudes in this neighborhood don't do squat but cause trouble. Just promise me you'll make another one, kapeesh?"

Angelo released a small smile and responded, "Maybe I'll put you in it."

"That would be the balls, my man! You can make a character called Fat Tony or something. I can be Fat Tony!" he shouted with laughter.

Angelo shot him a quick grin and nodded.

"Thanks for these, I appreciate it."

"Fat Tony says your welcome," he said, now hacking up lungs and wheezing as he laughed.

A few days later on the way to the airport Angelo found himself parked in front of Kelly's parent's house, a movie poster in the passenger seat next to him. He had hoped they weren't going to be home but there was a car in the driveway so he sat and stared as he gathered his nerve. Letting out a deep sigh he popped open the door and stepped out.

After what seemed like hours, he made it to their front porch. He straightened his shirt and adjusted his posture. His hand slowly rose to finally knock and he winced.

"They're not there," a voice came from the sidewalk behind him. He turned to see a man in a robe holding a dog on its leash. "They left this morning. Told me to watch the place. They'll be back on Monday."

Relief washed over Angelo. His shoulders sunk and he rolled his neck.

"Thanks," he replied, raising the poster. "I'm just going to leave this here for them. It should be fine here for a few days."

The man nodded then waved and went on with his walk, looking back over his shoulder as if he recognized him from somewhere.

He was already wearing his festival badge when he boarded the plane. Once again excitement began to light up his nerve endings, this time mixed with anxiety and an uneasy stomach. He found his seat and adjusted his badge so everyone could see it but no one paid any mind.

A few hours later he realized how much he drank on the flight when he stumbled off the plane into a massive throng of shuffling bodies that filled the airport. He tried to focus his eyes on the terminal numbers before just asking a nearby worker. After finally making his way through the crowd he looked around for his Uber driver who was parked right in front of him and finally waved him down.

"You some sort of filmmaker?" the driver said on the way to the hotel, reading his badge from the rearview mirror. "Are they having some sort of festival or something?"

"No, well, yea I guess," he answered. "I was, I mean, I did make a movie once. A long time ago. They're having this thing for it."

"That's cool, what's it called?" Angelo was about to answer when the driver swerved hard to avoid hitting a car switching lanes without looking. "People these days. I can't believe it. Anyway, it's cool you made a movie. I usually know about festivals and conventions happening in town. Guess this one slipped through the cracks."

Angelo gave him a small grin and then just sat back and watched the city flow by in blurry, streaking images.

That night, deep in an alcoholic sleep, he saw Kelly. She floated in from the dark, her hair wisping around her face, hiding it from view but he knew it was her. She was speaking in low, muffled tones and all he could do was ask what she was saying, but his voice was merely sounds. No syllables. No clear words. But he felt fear. He reached for her hand but it turned to dust in his. When he looked up at her she was gone. But Angelo wasn't alone. Two white figures emerged from the dark where Kelly once stood. He could hear their words. Their harsh tones, angry curses. It was her parents. He could feel their spittle on his face before a hard blow across his face send him to the sound ground of the dark dream void. There was another, then another. He found himself weeping and pleading in desperate monotone hums for it to stop, but it didn't.

The next morning, he rushed out of his room with his trusty plastic box. His film was scheduled to be the first one to be shown and open the festival, so he made it to the theater early expecting the festival organizers to have a green room for him where he could mingle with other filmmakers. When he showed up to the venue the sidewalks outside were empty. He readjusted his box of merch then looked up and saw his name on the marquee. He took out his phone and snapped a selfie in front of it.

Any nervousness that tugged on his guts was blown away when he opened the door and a massive crowd rushed to great him. A small man walked up, nodded and took his container. People were taking pictures, posing with him, shoving things in his hands to sign and laughing and cheering. It was a dizzying experience, but one Angelo had dreamed of. The flashes. The admiration. He felt famous, like he made it. He couldn't really see what was going on around him but he felt it all.

Eventually, a man pulled him away and ushered him into another room.

"Every movie eventually finds its audience, am I right?" the man said, dressed in a suit with slicked back hair and a big moustache. "I hope you found the theater okay?"

"Yes," Angelo answered breathing heavy. "This is pretty amazing. I mean – wow! Are they all here to see my movie?"

"It's the only movie playing at the festival."

"What? Really?"

"We know all about you and how you made the film – everything. We're all very, very big fans, my boy, and are so glad you traveled all this way to be here." Angelo couldn't believe this was all real and just laughed to himself. "Come, come. It's showtime."

He followed the man into the now empty lobby where he held open the door.

"Your fans await, sir," the man said tossing Angelo a prim and proper, yet peculiar smile.

The theater was pitch black once the door closed behind them. He tried to feel around when a gloved hand grabbed his and began leading the way. Nearly fumbling up some stairs he finally stopped when the hand released his.

A bright spotlight burst on and he realized he was on the stage of the massive theatre. He couldn't see anyone's features, but he could see hundreds of bodies filling the seats and balconies. He couldn't do anything but smile.

The small man came out and set a microphone stand in front of him and motioned for him to speak.

"Wow, um, jeez," he uttered. "This is, I mean, I couldn't have asked for more than this." The audience erupted in applause. "I won't keep you all from the movie but I just want to say thank you for coming." Applause filled the theater. "I also want to say that this is dedicated to the lovely Kelly Archer, who sadly passed away shortly after this movie was made. She just wasn't the main actress; she was the leading lady in my life as well." The crowd let out an echoing 'awwwwww' with some sniffles scattered throughout. "Thank you all so much and enjoy the show."

The light went out and it was pitch black again. The gloved hand found him and escorted him to his aisle seat. He slid into it and sat in complete silence with the audience. He bumped shoulders with the person sitting next to him and apologized.

"No worries," said a female voice, that sounded oddly familiar.

The movie began, filling the space with silver light and the crowd erupted yet again. Angelo looked around, taking it all in and grinning wildly. He watched the crowd as the opening credits rolled and his breath stopped. His grin faded.

The person across the aisle looked odd. Her skin was shriveled and wrapped tightly around her bones. The man next to her a dark empty socket on one side of his face. The person in front of them was dressed in vintage clothes, but they were ripped and dirty. Rotten fingers stuck out of filthy gloves. Further up there sat a torso with no head. In front of him was someone with just tufts of wild hair jutted out of an oozing skull.

He began to panic. He began to believe that this was all a dream. Or nightmare, he wasn't sure which. Angelo's jaw hurt as if he had been struck with a blow from his dream the night before. He began to squirm in his seat when a hand gently touched his arm. Leaping from his seat, he snapped his head over to see what creature had grabbed him.

But all he saw was Kelly, her kind blue eyes shimmering in the glow of their film.

"Kelly ...," he whispered, the person behind him putting their boney finger to their rotting lips in an attempt to shush him.

"Angelo, I'm really glad you came. I missed you so much," she whispered back. "Isn't this whole thing just so wonderful." Angelo, still staring at her in shock, just nodded. "Please, just relax and enjoy this. It's all for you. I thought you'd love it."

Angelo looked around at the audience, their eyes, if they had them, were locked on the screen. They laughed at the funny moments and screamed at the horror he had created. The crowd of corpses also cheered every time Kelly was on screen and she would bury her face in his shoulder.

Angelo sat back, gripped Kelly's hand, and enjoyed the show. Every minute of it. He knew this wasn't exactly how he expected it but loved it, nonetheless. He was with his love watching their movie, and even though he was surrounded by rotting corpses, it wasn't too far off from a comic book convention except the audience wasn't in costume. They were dead. But it was still kind of perfect.

And after the movie was over and the applause died down, they showed it again. And again. During the fifth screening Angelo finally noticed Kelly's parents getting up from the front row to leave. Their clothes were matted with blood and held blunt, dripping objects in their gloved hands.

Her father laughed. "Can you believe he fell for the fake film festival? Who would screen his film, much less buy him a plane ticket or hotel stay."

Years later, construction workers discovered a body inside that old, condemned theater. No one was sure who he was or where he came from, but when the building was set to be demolished, they found him sitting on the aisle seat. Just skin and bones, complete with a huge smile pulled across his leathery face.

He was holding a box filled with memorabilia from a movie no one had heard about.

Patterns of Light by Daniel Soliz

Roberta Shellum Dohse

Roberta Shellum Dohse hails primarily from California. She is a graduate of the University of California Berkeley. After a stint on a farm in northern Minnesota and time in Oregon, she moved to Texas in 1980. She attended law school at the University of Houston and has practiced law in Corpus Christi, Texas since 1997. She was formerly a flight instructor and a college professor. She has always loved to write.

A Cup of Tea Together

The China cups are ready,
England and Japan.
Translucent to the light,
So fragile in my hand.

Three teapots to be filled
Orange pekoe, mint, Earl Grey.
Shortbread cookies, petit fours,
Just waiting for the day.

The day that you come home
Your journeys then all run.
Tell me of your travels
Until the day is done.

We'll laugh and cry together
The way we used to do,
Share the pictures, paint our lives
In colors old and new.

If I were a sailor
We would cross the ocean wide,
But I'm happy having tea, so long
As you are by my side.

Sea Glass

The night you left the storm came in.
Waves crested so high
Pounding the shore
Tearing the sand from under my feet
Pulling it back into the undertow
As wild rain pelted
Nearly horizontal
And scoured the sky.

Boats tossed madly
In their moorings
Straining against their ropes
And the cliffs appeared
And disappeared
Emerging only to dissolve
Back into the swirling clouds
Again and again.

It was as if broken
Chords of my piano
Had taken flight and cracked
Through the air to crash
Against my mind,
Against my disbelief.
And I watched myself splinter
Into a thousand shards of glass.

And I blew through the wind
And into the sea
Where I was driven into sand
Pounded on the shore
And light was refracted in entirely new ways.
Sharp edges ground down, smooth to the touch,
No longer translucent
But resilient, frosted sea glass.

Robin Carstensen

Robin Carstensen is the Coordinator of the Creative Writing program Texas A&M University-CC where she advises *The Windward Review*: literary journal of the South Texas Coastal Bend, and is co-founding, senior editor of the *Switchgrass Review*: literary journal of health and transformation. *In the Temple of Shining Mercy* was awarded an annual first-place award by Iron Horse Literary Press and published in 2017. Poems are also published in *BorderSenses, Southern Humanities Review, Voices de La Luna, Selena Anthology* (forthcoming), and many more.

The Hold

Comes pouring you into wakefulness,
the fuschia bougainvillea fluctuating its arms,
heart on all sleeves, embroidering its bright
exotic gestures all down the chain link
fence flanking the overgrown and falling
neighborhood park as you drive past
on your way home from work. You remember
the sheer drop if not the actual distance
in which you will someday be cut off
from this event, and every other, each kiss
of the planet, this fireball, this molten cave's
echo where you've puffed heavy smoke
rings, leaned back in your mammoth chair
like a man—leg crossed with foot on knee,
drunk whiskey straight into dawn under
a stuffed boar's head, where still you drew
slowly the big-hearted rivers, and they flowed
past your prime, unfolding all you could
hope for, and didn't they always, all the apertures
for breathing whisper to hang on. You were
healing your mortal wounds, that's why it took
so long to arrive, and how could you be farther
ahead, when you've been trickling from your own
fissures and pores like a rivulet once walled
and bound, shedding the violence of should,
you were hanging on with your best imitation,
you were ice picking up your cosseted crags,
ascending every impasse subtly here, flamboyantly
there, indulging your various appetites for raw

innards, your palate for curried fish or malt barley
grist—old world bitters—you've been cruel
to yourself, you've been beautiful, you, becoming
so close, suspended by everything gossamer—
this airy mystery and lyric mesh—holding on
your whole life, each pungent flash, and always,
like these papery bracts, on the edge of falling.

Originally published in *Terrain.org*

Parade Rest

One potato had fed three brothers and her some nights D-Day sirens raided their dreams. Deutschland rebuilt itself in months, trusting authorities still, efficiency more. Mother was an expert quilt-maker artfully guiding each stitch. She was your father's liebchen, you could not learn her patience for sewing—how to follow her lithe hands, some days hard, ascetic strokes.

Father, young lieutenant, waded through rice paddies in Tam Quan, saw his commander's head blown off. The head of a good man with a compass and convictions. A family in his pocket gleaming from worn edges of amber grain and honey. Shell shocked, father stepped in, dragged the men from hills and bowels, jumped from planes at nine thousand feet.

Rhineland and Airborne Rangers held the reins to survival, to follow the rules, you might not die. What could you hear above their voices, ricocheting through the house and your minor indiscretions. Your skin standing at full attention when they called your name, every pore open, follicles quivering on edge, never quite at parade rest.

***

You at 16, a crawling feline, flat to the ground under barbed wire, knotted taut around the red two-story brick quarters lined up like good foot soldiers guarding Fort Monmouth, New Jersey, your hormones roiling for a Tomcat, the noncommissioned officer's son residing a few blocks off post in noncommissioned officer housing. You, a silent howl in summer's gorged heat.

Mother's Hummel figurines going about their quiet pastoral duties, you tearing out into midnight climbing, rolling wire fence under the gaping moon and the military complex, the unguarded long run and reconnaissance beneath the glistening innocence clamping down in the wet-slick thickening night, mysterious terrains, hands and mouths fluttering like doves and silk scarves.

Your body a ribbon floating home at dawn back over barbed wire, slipping into the brick barrack-attic, avoiding each floorboard creak up the narrow steps where your Father had entrusted you to the private room. What did you know of the guards stationed at the gates instead of perimeters for insurgents, your narrow escape from court martial or the firing squad

in the House of the Airborne Ranger Mother and Father, now at parade rest, who had climbed up through the dense forests of Giessen, North Dakota, Vietnam, through fire and brimstone, their arms full of men and approval, children, ropes, quilts, a dachshund, and hand grenades.

Sarah K. Lenz

Sarah K. Lenz is an essayist, poet, and English instructor at Del Mar College. In 2019, she founded the Writers' Studio, a community-based literary education center. debut essay collection, *What Will Outlast Me?* will be published by Unsolicited Press, Summer 2023.

Driving the Section Line

"When I die, I want you to dump my ashes on Henry's Hill," Dad said. We sat at his kitchen table in his trailer house on lot #1, Del Mar Mobile Home Court, in Doniphan, Nebraska, where he now lived alone.

"Okay," I said. "Why are you telling me this?"

"Someone needs to know." He had a USA Gold cigarette—the brand he switched to when Marlboros got too expensive—pinched between his leathery fingers. His other hand clasped a can of Old Milwaukee red label. On the table a scrape the size of a dinner plate marked the spot where, decade after decade, he had rested his beer. Like a cataract or a contusion, the Formica's wood print had been scraped down by the bottom of the can.

"Now, I mean it. You're to cremate me and dump my ashes on Henry's Hill."

He had reached the familiar state of drunkenness in which he repeats himself, forgetting moments ago what he just said. He would reiterate this thread of conversation over and over, until he ran out of beer or stumbled off to bed to pass out. I took a sip of my beer. It was late May, and I was back from grad school in Georgia for a visit. I only saw Dad once or twice a year, and as much as it was tedious to sit there in the same conversation loop, something in me felt duty bound. My husband, Kent, had stayed behind in Georgia. I'd called him earlier that afternoon because I needed to tell someone about how depressing it was to see how my dad's life had diminished. Kent reminded me: "You're the best thing he's done. He's proud of you and loves you. You can handle this visit." Though I appreciated his words, filial obligation weighed heavy. I thought about my younger sister who hadn't spoken to our father in over a decade, not since he showed up to her wedding drunk. Part of me envied her for the clean break she'd made.

"The kitchen looks nice," I offered, trying to get him out of the conversational rut. Since my last visit, he'd remodeled, put in new oak cabinets and shiny laminate floors.

"It was a bitch putting that sink in," Dad said, waving his beer can toward the new stainless-steel fixture. "I broke two sets of brackets, had to make three trips to Menards. Looks pretty good, though. Sandy picked it all out before she got sick." He paused, took another long swig of beer. "Dump my ashes on Henry's Hill. You got that?"

"Yes, you already told me." I wished Sandy was here. She'd been Dad's girlfriend. The last time I saw her we sat at this same table drinking Diet Dr. Pepper (her favorite). She told me: "Your father doesn't have a malicious bone in his body. Sure, he drinks, but he wouldn't hurt a flea." She lived with him until she got sick last winter. A kidney infection had turned into sepsis, and she'd spent three weeks in the ICU. When I was visiting for Christmas last year, Dad had taken me to see her in the hospital. Because of the excruciating pain she was in, the doctors put her in a medically induced coma. I thought back to how heartbroken I had been for my dad that day.

"Sandy, it's me, Rolland. Sarah's here too," he said as he leaned over her hospital bed. He gently brushed her mussed hair from her forehead and gave her a kiss. Her eyes fluttered open for a moment, but I'm sure they couldn't register what they saw. His eyes filled with tears. When he saw me watching him, I looked away, focusing on the coloring book pages hanging listlessly around the room, which Sandy's grandkids had brought.

When we left the hospital, it was brutally cold. The wind blew full tilt from the north, rattling the flagpole's rope and pulley. In the car, Dad tamped a cigarette from his pack and lit it. My breath streamed out in cloudy wisps, mingling with his cigarette smoke.

He finally spoke, "It sure is hard to see her like that, isn't it?"

I nodded. Afraid that he was going to cry again, I stared at the empty parking space next to us where someone had dropped a banana peel. Splayed flat across the frozen asphalt, its blackened edges curled in on itself in frozen helplessness.

"Hey, get me another beer, will ya?"

I got up from the table. Though there was a whole case of Old Milwaukee in his fridge, there was little food. A crumpled McDonald's bag with half a burger inside sat on one shelf, a dozen eggs and a package of hotdogs on the another.

"Do you miss Sandy's cooking?" I asked as I handed him a beer.

"Everyday." He belched, then cracked the new beer open and slid the tab sideways, a gesture I have seen him repeat hundreds, if not thousands of time.

The next day, Dad and I went on what he called "his nostalgia tour." We headed north for 60 miles, driving his twenty-year-old Geo Prizm, and ended up in Geranium Township at the top of Henry's Hill. Supposedly it was the highest point in Valley County. We stood at its summit, just before the elevation dropped off into a ravine. A rotten fence post covered with lichen jutted from the earth, trailing a curl of rusted barbed wire. A few orange cedar trees and smaller clumps of spiked yucca dotted the pasture. From that vantage we saw what used to be our homeplace, 160 acres of farmland that—until my father lost it—had been in the Krahulik family for five generations, since 1903.

The two-story farmhouse, red barn, and grain bins occupied a quarter-mile section. We took in the expanse of cornfields and feedlots full of cattle, all the land that used to be his. It was a geographical center. Point your finger at the middle of Nebraska on a map; you'll land on it. It was my father's center, too. As if by gravity or some other invisible force, he was pulled there now, even decades later. I imagined shaking his ashes from an urn, and how they would scatter on the wind and land on the soil he used to plow.

"Here's the spot."

"Is it legal?" I asked Dad, wondering about who owned the land, about trespassing laws and burial laws.

"Better to ask forgiveness than permission."

He flicked his cigarette down off the embankment, giving me something else to worry about. The combination of dry wind and parched grass was perfect for brush fires. The wind made a high-pitched groaning as it swept over the cottonwoods and made me feel spooked. It had a sinister quality, unlike any place I had ever lived, not like the soupy humid air of the Deep South, nor the arid air Idaho's foothills. Those places didn't have real wind, unlike here where the weather was mercurial.

"When'd you start farming?" I asked.

"Let's see, that would have been spring of '77." He squinted into the distance between the pasture and cornfields. He didn't see well anymore and needed cataract surgery. "Get me those binoculars in the glove box, will ya?"

He had parked the white Geo a few feet away in the empty hay field. I got the binoculars for him.

"I should have known I'd have bad luck," he continued, binoculars held tight against his eyes as he focused in on the homeplace. "That first year, corn got hailed out. Lost everything." Then he paused, set the binoculars down. "That kind of thing makes it hard not to be superstitious. Makes you wonder about God."

To read the rest of "Driving the Section Lines" with Sarah's original photography, use your smartphone to scan the QR code.

Shannon Dougherty

Shannon Dougherty has English and creative writing degrees from Southern Methodist University and the University of Texas at Austin. Her poetry has appeared in *Acorn*, *Modern Haiku*, *Oyster River Pages*, *The Chaffin Journal*, and *Corpus Christi Writers 2019*. She has lived in Corpus Christi since 2004.

Unknowns

Seagulls funnel over the houses crying
hush of kittens in the weeds
ears folded, blind to her returning.

Soft as the air, doves in the early dark calling
scent of mystery, nameless tree
fifth day flowering.

To be a post of the pergola standing
a part holding up the whole
a plank in a deck belonging

I might leave the earth if I flexed this feeling,
my bones to the weeds to weave
and the lattice to fall like all my trying.

But there were the cats breeding, the weeding and the mowing
the rust, rot, and salt that ate
what the insects left.

If I never had this, would I miss it?
Had I never stood here,
would I be missing?
No knowing.

S.P. Wilkins

S.P. Wilkins is a native of Corpus Christi. Over 80 of her creative non-fiction articles appeared in *Metro Leader Newspaper* and *The Bend Magazine*. She holds an MFA in Creative Writing and English from Southern New Hampshire University and is a member of the Writers' League of Texas. She works as an online English and writing tutor for Southern New Hampshire University.

Read The Reviews

It's not that the piano teacher is unqualified—bless her for still trying to play after losing that finger—but that she cares more about making money than teaching any discernible piano skills. Four weeks into our lessons and I still don't know the difference between middle C and E-flat. Alright, that's not entirely true. One's a white key and the other is black.

Her teaching philosophy seems to be based on an amalgam of knowledge gleaned from Wikipedia and YouTube. She tried telling us—Oh, I'm sorry! I forgot to mention this is a group piano lesson. Forty-five minutes. Six students. No discount for siblings. See what I mean about money. And it's not like I have a lot to spare. Do you have any idea how much it cost me to purchase Ludwig van Beethoven's teeth?

Anyway, for our first lesson, she threw out words like *re dièse* and *semitone* and *solfège*, which I later learned are all from the first sentence of the Wikipedia description of D-sharp. Information useless to a beginner pianist and free for those with internet access. Prior to my awareness of her sources, though, she dazzled us with those fancy French-sounding terms and a brightly-colored, spiral-bound book, which she held out like a trophy to be admired. Written by none other than the piano teacher herself, she spent thirty of our forty-five minutes singing its praises. Well, not really singing. She's a piano teacher, not a voice coach.

She rattled off a list of prior students who all achieved fame thanks to her book, and lamented the few who refused to let her help them ascend to greatness. Parents leaned in as she spoke, their expressions a mix of eagerness and greed.

The price of this holy grail of piano lessons? $49.99

Surely your child's future is worth a mere $49.99?

Those hesitant with their credit cards were quickly shamed into making a purchase. The piano teacher was allegro with her implications—if you didn't buy the book, you didn't care about your child's future.

As the only adult in this beginner piano class, I didn't have to worry about my non-existent child's fate. I left the lesson with my $49.99 (plus tax) intact, excited at the prospect of putting fingers to ivory the following week.

Lesson two wasn't any more informative, although this time we were presented with a visual of a piano. A piano being played in a YouTube video. That's right. I paid sixty dollars to watch YouTube in a stranger's home. Why didn't I leave? Well, it clearly states in the contract I signed that the piano lessons, which had to be paid in advance, are non-refundable. Plus, this was only lesson two. I still believed I would procure my musical education.

The piano teacher raved about the pianist's technique, her praise a cadence as he concluded his performance. She claimed to have taught him herself. Her strategic placement in front of the video username seemed accidental. It wasn't until after our third lesson, once I began my research, did I discover that the piano virtuoso not only did not have a connection to the piano teacher, but he was a child prodigy who had taught himself.

Lesson three began promising enough. There was an actual upright piano sitting in the middle of the room. It glowed with a promise. A promise of divine music. Electronic keyboards were stationed around it—three on each side. This was it, this was going to be the actual piano lesson.

We were instructed to select a keyboard. Giddy with excitement, I chose the one closest to me. It was positioned so it faced the keys of the upright piano—the piano from which I expected the piano teacher to elicit notes so beautiful we couldn't help but be inspired.

The piano teacher walked around the room, confirming keyboards were switched on. Then, she took her position in front of her piano. She raised her hands, glanced first to her left and then her right, and slammed her fingers down onto the keys.

Cats in heat are more musical than the caterwauling that emanated from that tortured instrument.

As the wailing grew to crescendo, she bid the rest of us to join her.

Feel the music! Become one with the keys!

Five different electronic howls joined the fray. I reached to my ears to check for bleeding.

This wasn't music. This was a violent assault on my auditory processes.

The piano teacher flung her head back and swayed as she surrendered to a melody only she could hear.

I glanced around the room, expecting to meet angry faces as parents realized they had been scammed.

To my surprise, every adult—save me—was grinning. I learned later that, in her $49.99 book, the piano teacher had promoted this lack of teaching as an actual technique! Well, I was not to be fooled. I decided to spend my time between this lesson and next investigating the proficiency of the piano teacher.

My hours of searching revealed a sordid tale of one star reviews and an F rating from the Better Business Bureau—not that she was a member. Had I been physically able to, I would have kicked myself. My eagerness to finally fulfill my life-long dream of learning to play the piano had deterred me from my usual tactic of researching before spending. Let my tale be a lesson for you—always read the reviews.

You know how lesson four went. This time we were to sit silently on the floor and stare at our keyboards. We had to absorb the musical energy harnessed in those circuits before we could truly begin to learn how to play. I had expected this, having followed the white rabbit down the internet hole to the piano teacher's failings.

So, why did I go back? Why did I drive the thirty minutes to sit in a stuffy living room furnished with worn leather sectionals from the seventies and not learn how to play the piano? Well, Officer, love makes you do funny things, and I loved hearing her fortissimo scream as I sawed off her finger.

S. Matt Read

From 2009 to 2010, S. Matt Read hiked around the perimeter of Texas, clocking about 3,200 miles. This story is from Day 67.

In the Presence of Witches

I'm walking northeast along Highway 43 toward Caddo Lake State Park. This is East Texas, and it's steamy. The pines stand tall all around me like the sides of a pot. I'm cooking slowly, the sweat burning my back, neck, and the corners of my eyes. I dodged some torrential rains a few days ago by holing up with Richard Hollingsworth, a Presbyterian minister and childhood friend of my father's. Even though the rains are behind me, the humidity is just getting started. I'm already thinking of a midday break.

I am grateful to Richard for his company. These first couple of months have really worn me down. I ended an eight-year relationship right before coming out here, and the decision's left me off balance. I question everything now. Who am I? What am I doing out here? It's an endless parade of thoughts, and my mind gives me no rest.

To keep occupied, I've been making wikiups the last two nights. These are simple, makeshift shelters using branches and leaves. Think Ewok chic. For the first, I found a mostly horizontal downed tree with space underneath and leaned several branches against it. For the second, I placed branches flat over a pit and threw leaves on top, creating a little pit-home in the earth. Even standing a few feet away, a person would have had a hard time spotting me. If I have time, I'll make a third tonight.

So I'm walking along and see a perfect hill for my break. A cluster of pines near the top is all the invitation I need. I hike up, put my pack down, and get out makings for a peanut butter and apple sandwich. I never had these as a kid and only recently started enjoying them. The bread isn't squished, which is good, and the peanut butter is super hot and liquidy because of the heat. I drink a little to kick off my meal.

Where I'm seated, I can see a home across the street. A woman and a man come outside and exchange a few words. It feels like something is happening. The man goes inside and comes out with a rifle. I'm reading but am also glancing up, watching whatever this is unfold. He gets into a four wheeler, comes down the driveway and into the street, goes just a few yards down to another driveway, and disappears. I think this is fairly unusual. Then again, I'm hiking around Texas.

A few minutes pass.

I see the woman walk up to her fence. She's got dark hair and tanned arms, but her face is obscured by a pair of binoculars. With these trained on me, she yells out, "Hey there! Whatcha doing?" I yell back,

"Just having lunch!" After a few more yells back and forth, I put down my book, leave my stuff, and walk down the hill for an easier conversation. She keeps those binoculars on me right until the street. I don't see the man.

"You're just walking through?" she asks me. I assure her I am and explain the trip. "Well, I told my son to get a closer look at you. I told him, 'If he does anything funny, just shoot him!'" I don't know what to say to this. The son appears off in the distance near the house, but gratefully, the gun is nowhere in sight.

This lady doesn't seem to notice my discomfort. She explains they've been robbed a number of times. Even the dog got stolen. According to this woman who gave her son the greenlight to shoot me, the entire area has gone to pot.

Our conversation is pleasant enough, aside from the casual death threat, and she even offers to refill my water. I decline and shove off, going up the hill again to pack my things.

The last few miles to Caddo Lake State Park vanish quickly. I register at the main office for a tag, and when it comes to the spot where I have to choose either car or bicycle, I draw my own box with "walked" beside it. I save two bucks.

It's early, so I decide to make my third wikiup. I want it large, big enough for me and my backpack. There's nowhere to hide here, not like my second spot, so it sticks out from the rest of the car campers. It's like a witch moved into Caddo Lake.

Night comes quickly. I eat a warm just-add-water evening meal and admire my handiwork. Then I clean up, brush, and get inside. I'm pretty sure I'll fall asleep quickly, but I don't. The heat doesn't help. I stay up, just listening to the night sounds, trying to get comfortable.

Then I hear a car pull up. The campers are not shy about yelling to each other across the pitch blackness. It seems they've lost a kitten. I roll my eyes at this, and just listen some more. Lots of "I see it"s and "Get it"s. I see flashlight beams through the cracks of my wikiup, as they tromp around the entire area.

One of the campers wanders close to my spot and stops yelling. It's clear he's seen the witch's den. This would be the perfect moment to come out yelling and screaming, but I hold back. He wanders away, and the group finds the kitten soon after. They set up their tents noisily, and eventually let the peace back in. I get to sleep after midnight.

I'm up early the next day. I'd like to leave the wikiup standing, but a ranger let me know that I needed to leave the site the way I found it. I tear it down and disperse the limbs, leaves, and pine needles into the surrounding forest. It's time for this witch to move on.

As I leave, I'm thinking that's probably going to be my last wikiup for a while. Here then gone – like thoughts, like kittens, like everything.

Susan Daubenspeck

Susan Daubenspeck has been writing poems since she was 15 years old. Poetry has been her lifeline. She retired a few years ago after 25 years as an Oncology nurse here in Corpus and in Houston.

Egypt Via Sunset Cove

Because my daughter, Emily, had moved to Saudi Arabia two years earlier to teach second grade on an American/European compound and because I had recovered from a nearly year long debilitating illness, I accepted her offer of sharing an Egyptian vacation – 8 days in Cairo and Luxor.

On the last leg of the flight from Houston to Cairo I nodded off again. I'd been cat-napping for about fifteen minutes every few hours. My plan for five or six good hours of sleep was thoroughly done in by the "jet lag monster" who hides like a lost shoe under cramped seats on jumbo jets and eats up one's sense of time.

I dreamt of a golden door. And Ra, Sun god of ancient Egypt, was there to meet me. A nice gesture I was thinking when BOOM!...I was in a boat on Sunset Cove. I knew it was Sunset Cove from a sign I'd just passed. "SUNSET COVE, Idaho", it read. I'd never heard of it but there I was in the middle of it. The wind was like a silk scarf blowing in my face veiling my eyes. Then it dropped away and across the lake on the shore I saw a small child, a boy, who threw his arms up in supplication.

I know that's a heavy and loaded word but there it was. A cartoon circle over the boy's head spelled out "SUPPLICATION." He could have been my brother, Bobby, who had died as a toddler. Or my son, a bright spot in my life. Maybe he was a symbol of hope for our young (and usually dumb) human species. He could have been something else. Or none of these at all.

The young woman seated next to me nudged me awake.

"Look out your window," she urged.

I opened my eyes and did. Peaks of the Gaza pyramids were rising up to greet us as our plane started to circle Cairo. I felt the boat on Sunset Cove turn also and putter towards another shore. The sun was shining like a halo, a round golden door.

We landed safely in Cairo. As I deplaned I remembered it was my birthday.

Theresa Kuhl-Babcock

Theresa Kuhl-Babcock has worked for over two decades as a Masters Level School Psychologist (LSSP) in Texas. Living a full life traveling, adventuring and raising a family in addition to experiences gained through her professional life are all in the scope of her creative pursuits. *Not Quite Broken* is her first and only published novel, set in Corpus Christi. The short story contributed in this compilation is another emotional and insightful piece meant to touch the heart and raise empathy of readers.

Empty

Staying in the present drains the life right out of me. The current negative moment is that our son Corey is going off to college, and I am about to be an empty nester. My chest aches with the knowledge that while I can create a new truth, my past represents the best of times and the worst of times.

He walks in the door. "Hey mom. Did you make anything for dinner?"

"No. I figured you would just grab something." I'm not lazy, but both of my kids have preferred quick meals for some time. I've learned that the effort isn't worth it.

"Okay. Can you cook something tomorrow?" He's a charming eighteen-year-old with wild curly red hair and smile that just warms my heart.

I would love a family meal, even though he'll likely make a a plate and get online with his friends. Still, I take the bait. "I can make fajitas."

"Perfect. And I also want beef tips before I leave."

He lopes away, and I follow him to his dirty musky-smelling room with clothes and fast-food wrappers strewn everywhere. None of this is acceptable per our house rules, but unless I nag or do it myself, the mess is my reality. But not for long. Soon the room will be a hollow shell, just like the room across the hall. Chloe left for college two years ago. To distract myself from these thoughts, I begin picking up his things. "Did you turn in the check for your cap and gown?"

"Stop mom! I don't need you to clean my room." He rushes to pick up his clothes.

He is a sweet boy. I mean man. "Okay, I can make you a little something."

"Thanks." He gives me a peck on the forehead while towering over me to shut his door.

Tears nearly roll down my checks as I think about only having one more week in my parenthood journey. Chloe told me when she was 16 that parenthood doesn't stop when you graduate. She reassured me she would need me forever. Now that she is 21, off in college, I hear from her every few months. The phone calls are like a jolt of electricity, that depletes me to zero when the connection ends. The connection ends, yes, that is how it feels. When they go, the connection ends.

The dogs begin barking. My husband, Ryan, walks in with a stack of who knows what in his arms and puts them on the front table. "Hey!" he says, but he's already walking into the bedroom to change and does not expect an answer. Our lives are so routine, predictable, lackluster. When you mold your life around your children, that is what happens.

While I contemplate my emptiness, Ryan comes in wearing his tight red Aero Jersey ready for cycling. "I should be home around 7:30." He kisses me on my forehead. I remember when we use to give passionate kisses before parting. I remember so much. I miss so much.

"Have fun." I smile and goose him playfully.

"You know, you should really join me."

I want to say that this is the last week Corey will be here, and he should spend the time with us. But I don't. "Go." He means well, but he also knows that I hate cycling and would need years to gain the stamina needed to keep up with his riding group.

Our life together has been exactly this. Ryan filled his life with hobbies, while I took care of all the details. The kids over the last 21 years were the bulk of that burden. A burden that filled me with love, exhaustion, pride, and, at times, frustration. Regardless of good or bad moments, those moments were meaningful and became the clothing I wore to present myself to the world.

In a week, I will be naked. There is nothing worse than landing naked and full of shame. Shame that I am not stronger, more independent, more fulfilled within myself.

One week later, Chloe arrives to drive up with us to University of Texas. The Tahoe is full and my life is officially empty. Today may actually be the death of me.

"You're going to love it in Austin," she says. "I bet I'll even run into you at the drag." She looks like a model with her long flowing strawberry blonde hair billowing across her forehead. She is wearing a moss green crop top and baggy mom jeans with a large belt working hard to keep them over her non-existent hips. I used to have that figure.

"Don't cramp my style. Let me know before you creep around." He pushes her with his shoulder.

"Whatever, loser. You wish a girl as gorgeous as me wanted to creep on you."

Corey makes a gross face, "You are my sister!"

While they talk a big talk, they are actually very close and will be there for each other. Every part of me wants to sell the house and follow them, but I have been expressly forbidden from moving within 100 miles of UT.

"This is it," Ryan says as we pile into the Tahoe. "Our final road trip as the Charles family."

While my soul recoils at his words, Corey and Chloe begin chanting, "Road trip. Road trip." No part of me wants to begin the end of my life as I have defined it for twenty-one years.

Despite my silent emotional protest, the drive begins.

"Do you guys remember our road trip to Tennessee?" Ryan asks the kids, I mean the adults in the backseat.

"Yeah, mom read us *Diary of a Wimpy Kid.*" Corey goes on. "I read that whole series after that trip. Did you bring a book today, Mom?"

"Not today. I wish I had thought of it." The mommy of 15 years ago would have thought of it. But today I allow this moment to pass uneventful. Focused on tomorrow. Focused on the loss. No longer focused on the journey.

"I remember the cabin in the Smokey Mountains. Adults upstairs and kids downstairs. I had such a crush on your friend's kid. What was his name?" Chloe asks.

"Jeffrey. He was four years older than you." I respond.

"He was hot. That is what I remember." She was always a little boy crazy. Interestingly enough, she has grown into a very independent woman and has not yet brought home a serious boyfriend.

Corey changes the subject, "We went ziplining for the first time. I was the first one to go."

"You were scared. I think you just wanted to get it over with." Ryan is as nostalgic as the rest of us.

"True. I hated all the camping and exploring we did in boy scouts then, but now I love it. Lake Travis has a great zipline. We plan to go in few weeks after we get settled."

I imagine Ryan is feeling much like me. The exploring that used to be Daddy-time has transformed into the prerogative of a young man and his friends. I reach over and hold Ryan's hand. He gives me a knowing glance. My heart wrenches. Never have I wanted to turn back time more than today.

"We should plan a family trip over Christmas." Ryan offers.

Chloe looks guilty, "I already have a plan to go to Houston with Desi. I do plan to come down for Christmas Eve, but I have to be back the day after Christmas for work."

Desi? She has mentioned him a few times, but evidently he is a serious boyfriend—the first. Ryan and I exchange glances.

Corey joins in. "I don't want a big trip. That will be my first Christmas away. I want to take it easy and decide when it gets closer."

His first, coincides with my last. My last Christmas with parent authority passed without my really noticing. From here on out, my holidays will be at their will. Why did I let them become such independent healthy adults?

"I guess Mom and I can just take a trip by ourselves." Ryan gives me a suggestive wiggle of his eyebrow.

My chest tightens. Not because I wouldn't enjoy a trip with Ryan, but because I am in mourning. Mourning the death of my immediate family. Ryan and I are now extended family. How many times did I choose not to visit my parents? Instead, I happily created my own family. Would Corey and Chloe do the same and visit less and less? Leaving me waiting for the few and far between visits. I turn my head to avoid anyone noticing the lone tear running down my cheek.

Before we know it, we are at the dorm. Corey's journey into adulthood is starting. Sending your first off to college is hard but saying goodbye to your last is unbearable.

I focus on the tasks of the day. Unloading the car, decorating the room, eating lunch, and picking up the last few items from Walmart. The inevitable moment approaches. Slowly the wind dies, the streaks of sunshine disappear, the dark cloud rolls in, and the ominous truth enters without invitation. The time has come.

"Well, I guess this is it." Corey is excited and ready for us to leave. The juxtaposition of his happiness and my distress creates tension.

Ryan pats me on the shoulder. "I guess we should leave. We are so proud of you. Don't forget about us and remember if you need anything, we are a phone call away." He hugs Corey enveloping the six-foot-tall man in his arms.

Chloe chimes in, "Don't worry. I am ten minutes away."

I can't speak. My body feels heavy, and my eyes are filled with sadness. Corey and Chloe look at me. I stick out my lower lip and mom up. "I love you, both. I wish I could take you home forever, but I did my job. Like Dad said, I am here if you need me." After a group hug, Ryan and I get in the Tahoe and drive away. I turn to look back but as quickly as the day started is as quickly as the moment ended.

In the empty car.

Empty.

portrait of Greg by Jimmy Peña
Jimmy's work is featured in The Cheech Marin Center

Portrait of Tom by Jimmy Peña

Tom Murphy

Tom Murphy is the 2021-2022 Corpus Christi poet laureate. He is also the copy editor for the *Corpus Christi Writers* series. His work has been published in *Langdon Review, Red River Review, San Antonio Express News, Texas Poetry Calendar, Centrifuge, Nebula, Strike, Switchgrass Review, Voices de la Luna, Windward Review, Writing Texas, Boundless Anthology, Speak Your Mind: Woody Guthrie Poets, Corpus Christi Writers, Outraged, Beatitude: Golden Anniversary Edition, The Call of the Chupacabra,* and *The Great American Wise Ass Poetry Anthology*. His latest books are *Pearl* and *Snake Woman Moon,* and *When I Wear Bob Kaufman's Eyes* is forthcoming.

twilight of stardust

left
sixty seasons
to farm
experts
            claim
our twilight
                        stardust

crashing chaos
from here to
new maternity
                        hello
echo —   good
                                    night
Irene — we have drowned

ourselves

choke
firelight air
red sun beat down

and *you* — want
to fund the pigs
follow hallow voices
                              baby
shit's too real now

fan blades
in our face
space
we need to find
to say adios
MF — melting away
it's
twilight of
stardust
my friend
breathe
from the O_2 tank
goggles on
swim thin light
soil
ready to give no more
nutrients depleted
hangman's gonna
swing
through death's door
those pearly gates false
human fatalities
Covid
disease — helps us
preserve all that we
stole — ready your
self
for the
underground

Sun Ra's racy dance

echo tide reverberates dawn sky
triskelion lion picks her teeth, eyeballing
a next catch in coastal fog, trees, cypress,
redwood, mesquite, bent backwards, like
gimp at Barcelona's cathedral's unshaven legs.
Oh mama, frogs holding tacos in the air, why
do their medals hang sideways and swirl like
pasties in a hothouse bar? Sunlight dances over
hands unfit to shovel graves, but blisters pop
and burn. Did you see the coming garbage trucks?
How do you put your pants on when you're still
fetal bed dreaming viscous scenes of death?

Tuning

Rothko Radio tuned
listen to the color spectrum
unleash waves and particles
aural broad swaths
cantilcver bombardment
stucco the museum mind;
just shuffle along.

Burnt Orange in C Minor
Seurat triplets E♭ A♭ and B♭
A fanfare breathing vermilion
into the Overture quartet
Clifford Still whole notes sustaining G
through B♭ — Flaxen, Corn, Medallion
Bumblebee, Mustard, Tuscan Sun.
Cacophony of color
trills of Franz Kline
black clouds and lighting strikes
mellows to Barnett Newman's Stations
white — Jay DeFeo's tactile rose.
John Cage's 4:33—played a
plethora fan in the key of orange:
Sunrise, Candle Light, Orangutan, Melon,
Pumpkin, Papaya, Goldfish, Creamsicle,
Monarch, Ginger, Apricot, Salamander,
Basketball, Starfish, Tangerine, Mac and Cheese.

Pin drops.

An aqua timber speaks,
"Color of the world,
this is Rothko Radio."

Wayne Hankins

Wayne Hankins lives in Corpus Christi, Texas. He studied creative writing, painting, architecture, and computer science; he worked for 25 years as a systems & software engineer in flight simulation trainers. Photo and poem by Wayne Hankins

Seventy Years

Seventy laps around the sun seemed enough when younger.

Now done, I've become greedy and want many more
because I still find all of this intensely interesting.
Everything about it still fascinates me:
the art of everything, culture, food/drink, life forms,

the vast universe with all its celestial bodies and our small planet,
science, math, life, living,
humans
with our amazing minds, hearts, souls.

These Rainier cherries are small
my enjoyment of them large.

Drinking coffee may seem a small thing
I assure you it is not.

Birthday wishes may also seem a small thing
but were not received that way at all.

Savor your days
and the people that have been in them.

William Mays

William Mays is the editor of *Corpus Christi Writers.* This is an excerpt from his novel, ***George: The Final Days***, the last book in the ***Saga of George*** trilogy. Available on Amazon.

CHAPTER ONE

Crack, crack, crack.

His wife and his *petherá* were cracking pecans.

They scowled when he entered the kitchen. Had some old flame surfaced and made false accusations—or worse, true ones?

"What?" he asked in English.

He held the attaché case with the monthly bribe money at his side. They looked at it and kept cracking, their movements synchronized as if they were different appendages of the same being. Dressed in black, obviously mother and daughter, dark-haired and large-breasted, they looked like they belonged in a village with the donkeys braying outside and a church bell tolling in the distance.

"It's going to be five years," Maria said in Greek.

George stuck to English. "Five years?"

They cracked hard like they were smashing his nuts and waited for him to figure out what they wanted. It was like a fucking game show, and he didn't have the answer, not even a clue. Their air-conditioner, a top-of-the-line unit, pumped quiet, frigid air; coffee perked on the stove. Something, chicken, he thought, baked in the oven. Outside, in the withering heat, their gardener roared past on their John Deere riding mower, leaving a wake of grass blades on the acre of manicured lawn.

When the sound of the mower faded, his *petherá*—his mother-in-law—hissed like a rattlesnake. "Five years since my husband died.

It was a punch in the gut. Old dead Manoli had to be venerated on the five-year anniversary, and George—the mobster for a new age—should have remembered.

He slid into his chair at the head of the table. "This is an important event," he said in formal Greek to placate the old bat. The *petherá* had her place in the universe along with the serpents, mosquitoes, cockroaches, and the various assorted plagues and calamities. George accepted God's plan even though he did not understand it. "You're making baklavá for the five-year memorial."

Maria barely waited for the words to get out of his mouth. "We talked to the priest. We will have it this Sunday. Our daughters will come into town."

Few people deserved less fanfare than Manoli. Even his demise, a heart attack after gorging himself on lamb at a wedding and then dancing a fast *Kalamatianó*, left little to admire. "Of course, of course. I'll be back from Chicago by Friday, and I don't have anything to do this weekend. It will work fine. Just tell me what you need."

They knew he'd be back Friday, knew he had nothing to do over the weekend, knew how many times he'd take a crap and how many sheets of toilet paper he'd use. Why were they having this discussion? He popped a pecan into his mouth and waited for their next move.

Crack. Crack. Crack.

Maria went in for the kill. "We want a big celebration. Dinner and a party at the Zeus and Hera on Saturday night. We'll get Jimmy and the Corinthians to play all the old songs. You know how my father loved them. Then, the memorial at the church on Sunday and a meal here. We want to invite some of the Chicago relatives. My aunts and my brothers and the two Marias. And my *koumbára*. And her family, including her sisters. And if we invite them, then we have to invite Pano. I talked to his wife yesterday. She says he's not feeling well, but his doctor says he's fine and that he can travel down here. And if we invite him, then maybe we should invite Lazarus."

He smashed his fist on the table; pecans bounced into the air. "No, no, no. It gives me a headache thinking about a big party. They'll camp out here for days, smoke cigarettes, drink all my whiskey, clog our toilets. And we can't have Lazarus." The pecan caught in his throat, and he almost choked. "Lazarus tried to kill me. More than once. Have you forgotten? I will not allow him in this house."

"There's been peace for so long. He won't cause trouble at a church event." Her voice hardened. "It is the five-year memorial. How many more times will my father be dead for five years?" She paused. "We invited your mother. We called her at her ranch and told her she could bring her boyfriend."

They were pulling out all the stops.

"We invited your Uncle Nick too, but, you know, he can't come."

Nick had fled to Greece one step ahead of the Feds, leaving George the caretaker of the house and businesses, but they pretended he was just off for an extended vacation and always invited him to the big events.

Maria and his *petherá* laid their nutcrackers on the table and awaited his answer. He looked at the large icon of Christ Pantocrator on one wall and then at an equally large framed photo of Pano on the opposite wall. There could be no simmering family discord before the *Panayías* holiday, nothing to upset Nick or Pano. And most of all, there could be nothing to pique the interest of Lazarus, the scumbag convert. The anger pulsed in his temples.

"Sure, sure, go ahead. But not Lazarus. I will not allow him in our house."

"Anything you say. You know, if you're worried about him, you need a bodyguard. I always tell you to get one, and you never listen. And stop meeting Beto at the mall. Everybody knows you own an art gallery there. People think you're getting soft."

His *petherá* tapped her head with her finger. "Your brains are soft like yogurt."

READ THE FIRST THREE CHAPTERS AT
MAYSPUBLISHING.COM

Picture of a Rock by Justin Quintanilla

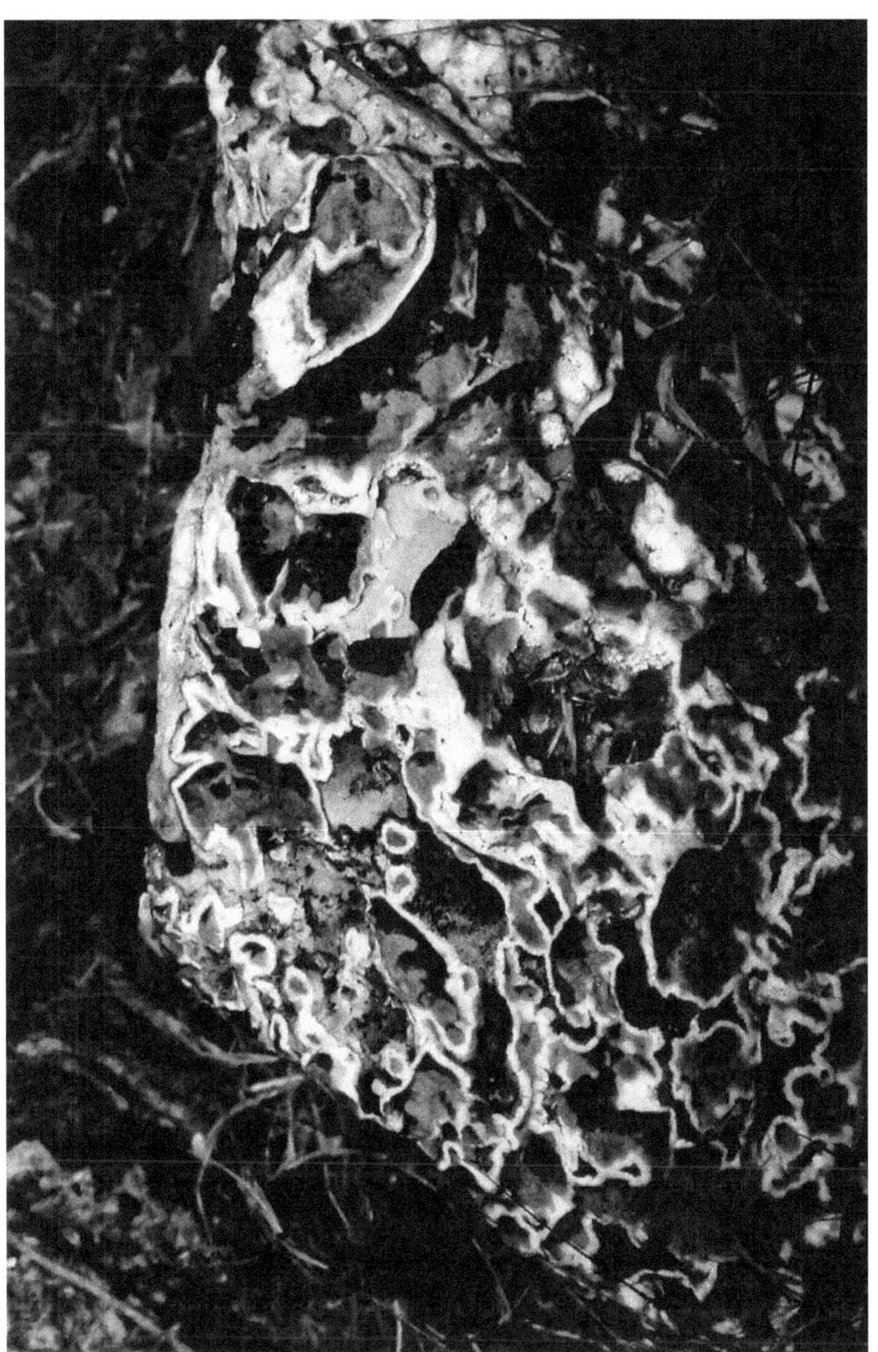

William Walton

William Walton grew up on a ranch in the Texas Hill Country. He graduated from Bandera Texas High School, then from Yale University. His stories have been published in several anthologies. His collected fiction is available in *Madmen and Fellow Travelers*.

Red Bird, Red Bird

Whomp!

What the crap was that?

Casey flinched, spilling hot coffee on his pajama pants.

Ouch!

Not the way he liked to start his morning. He set his coffee down and listened. After a couple of minutes of silence, he picked his cup up and took another sip.

Whomp!

Damn it.

Casey stood up and checked to see if he spilled coffee on the floor. Determining he hadn't, he sat back down. He cocked his head and listened.

Whomp!

Casey looked up toward the second floor loft. *Sounds like it's coming from the east window.*

He pushed himself up from his chair, paused for a moment, and made his way slowly up the stairs.

Whomp!

Upon reaching the loft, he walked over and stood a few feet from the window. He waited on unsteady feet, shifting his weight from one foot to the other.

Whomp!

From the loudness of the hits, he had expected at least a grackle, maybe even a hawk, but the culprit was, instead, a small red bird, a cardinal. Casey watched as the little bird made at least a half-dozen more hits, with short pauses between them.

Whomp!

Why in God's name...?

Then the banging stopped as abruptly as it began, and the red bird was gone.

The next morning Casey was pouring his first cup of coffee when the bird hit the window.

Whomp!

I'd like to finish my coffee with—

Whomp!

...without that damned bird banging on my window.

Casey put down the pot, exited the back of the house, and peered around the corner into a side yard. Almost immediately a flash of red movement caught his eye. His vantage point gave him a clear view of the cardinal perched on a tree branch about fifteen feet from the window. After a couple minutes of adjusting his position, the bird, with a sudden burst of energy, flew toward the window. At the last second, he pivoted his body so that he took the hit with his feet.

Whomp!

Immediately after impact, the bird fell a couple of feet toward the ground before recovering and flying slowly back to his tree branch.

Casey watched as the bird attacked the window at least a half dozen more times, with intervals of thirty seconds to a minute or two between hits. He was reminded of aberration of nature movies like Alfred Hitchcock's The Birds or Peter Benchley's Jaws. The bird's actions, too, seemed unnatural. If so, the cardinal appeared at peace with his situation. He stood on the tree branch, preened himself for a few minutes, and flew away.

The red bird was back the next morning.

Whomp!

Although Casey couldn't understand why the bird continued to come, he was unable to ignore it, to shut it out of his mind.

Whomp!

What is God's name does he want?

Whomp!

Red Bird, are you some kind of damned...?

Casey grabbed a broom, went outside, and slowly approached the bird's perch. He waved the broom back and forth, shooing the bird loudly until it flew off to a nearby tree. Casey pursued the red bird and repeated his actions, forcing it to retreat to an even more distant tree. Short of breath but satisfied, he turned and went back into the house.

Whomp!

Well, so much for scaring him away.

Casey put away the broom.

Whomp!

Damn it, that bird's gonna be the death of me.

That afternoon Casey drove to a hardware store and bought a plastic owl to frighten off the seemingly possessed cardinal. His hand shook when he tried to hang it, and it took him a couple of tries to get it in place. The bird was undeterred. The next morning it was back in full force.

Whomp!

Casey set down his coffee cup.

You stupid, friggin' bird, please—

Whomp!

...just go away and leave me alone.

The next morning the red bird did not come.

At first, Casey was relieved but then found himself listening for the bird, vaguely uncomfortable with its absence. After a week or so, he bought a bird feeder, filled it with seed, and hung it from the cardinal's favorite branch, but the bird did not return.

Every morning Casey brews his coffee, pours himself a cup, and listens for the bird. Sometimes, when his legs are strong enough, he climbs to the loft and waits by the window. This morning they weren't up to the task. On the way to his chair, he picked up a framed photo of his deceased wife and held it for a moment.

Red Bird, maybe you were...

He set the picture down, walked over to his seat, and lowered himself into it. He listened, but heard nothing.

Red bird, red bird, please...